The Jordan Experience

T. A. Boketon

THE JORDAN EXPERIENCE

Contents

Chapter	
Author's Dedication	vii
	viii

1	Becoming Ready – The Journey Before the Journey	1
2	Arrival and the Initial Two-Week Ordeal	6
3	Fear, Doubt, and Disclosure	17
4	The Reckoning	29
5	The Slow Healing and Counseling	41
6	The Turning Point	47
7	The Home Stretch	57
8	The Adventure	63
9	Adjusting to the Home Front	81
10	Coming Full Circle	87

Copyright © 2025 by T. A. Boketon

All rights reserved. No part of this book may be reproduced in any manner whatsoever without written permission except in the case of brief quotations embodied in critical articles and reviews.

First Printing, 2025

Written By:

T. A. Boketon

Published By:
Green Norton Publishing

The author dedicates this manuscript to those who have experienced sexual harassment in the workplace. This includes retaliation, intimidation, and passive-aggressive behavior directed at the person who was brave enough to report the incidents. The author understands that his firsthand accounts of what happened to him may cause others who have also experienced sexual harassment to feel anxiety and post-traumatic stress when recalling their experiences. Many may blame you, attempt to shame you, or disbelieve you, but remember you are not alone, and you did nothing wrong by inviting another person to sexually harass you.

1

Becoming Ready – The Journey Before the Journey

After years of contemplating whether to accept an overseas assignment with my employer, I decided to seize the opportunity in February 2023. I followed the proper process and nominated myself for a four-month overseas assignment. The decision to take this opportunity was admittedly complex. Professionally, I viewed an overseas assignment to deepen my understanding of field operations and gain firsthand experience that would boost my expertise as a Data Scientist. Additionally, the extra income from this assignment would help my spouse and me move closer to our goal of adopting an infant through a reputable agency. Some might see the latter motive as selfish, but it gave this hopeful man in his forties hope and optimism about becoming a parent with my partner, who is five years younger than me.

When I first shared my decision with my partner—who is now my spouse—in the spring of 2023, he encouraged me to confirm a tentative departure date. He also suggested we take an international trip beforehand to create memories before I left. The office managing the deployment told me that the earliest possible departure would be late 2023 or early 2024. Reassured, we moved forward with our travel plans for the year.

In May 2023, I received official notification by email that I had been selected for an overseas assignment, but this did not mean I would leave immediately. Instead, it indicated that I was on the rotation roster. The location where I would serve as a Data Scientist was Amman, Jordan. A few weeks after receiving the initial notice, I received a second email stating I was expected to start my overseas assignment in February 2024. This second email also introduced me to the agent who would guide me through all the necessary paperwork and training required before departing for my assigned overseas post.

By mid-June 2023, a wave of requirements started flooding my email inbox. Some materials felt urgent, while others could be delayed. However, the sheer volume of paperwork remained overwhelming. I immediately began to wonder if all the mandatory training and paperwork would be processed and approved on time! Things got even more stressful when I received additional paperwork giving me only two weeks to complete and schedule a meeting with an advisor for an official passport. The passport also needed to be expedited; if I did not receive it by mid-August, my overseas assignment would have to be postponed by another four months. I knew I did not want to delay by that much, so I worked meticulously and quickly to ensure everything was filled out and submitted on time—and, if possible, ahead of schedule. All the while, I kept thinking, This is ridiculous—last-minute notice!

Every agent I started communicating with assured me of the same thing, saying, "They have done this many times before, and despite the tight timelines, things always get completed, so do not worry." These agents were also quick to say that everything was expedited and arrived on time, provided I completed and submitted all paperwork correctly the first time. Fortunately, when I decided to go on my first overseas assignment, I had more than one coworker on my team who had already gone on an overseas assignment. These coworkers shared valuable knowledge about the process and knew how to fill out the forms correctly.

August arrived quickly! During that first week of August, my primary agent guided me through the overseas process and urged me to contact the agent handling my expedited official passport. After they confirmed it had been shipped, I received an email notification stating that the passport had arrived and was ready for pickup. Fortunately, the passport arrived just in time for my first of several pre-deployment training sessions. The initial training required shows the official passport as part of the verification process.

This initial mandatory training took place during the third week of August, a week after I received my official passport. It was an intensive week-long course held at an off-site location near Washington, D.C. The training was challenging. I learned how to manage active-shooter situations, biological and chemical terrorist threats, simulated escapes from overturned vehicles, and vital life-saving skills like wound cleaning and hemorrhage control, which could be crucial in an emergency.

On the first day of class, as the instructors showed us graphic images of what we might face, I started to worry about my ability to pass the course. These videos included both disturbing photos and real-world accident clips that demanded quick responses to stabilize victims and make sure they could reach a medical facility before losing too much blood.

Midway through the first day, I could not help but interrupt and mention that I was, in fact, afraid of needles and had been known to pass out, vomit, or both. I also added that I get nauseous from the sight and smell of blood, and I was worried this might be an issue in passing the course. As I said this aloud, I was also telling myself to get over it…the course is required for my overseas assignment. The instructors immediately and unanimously laughed, assuring me, saying, "No, that is not going to be a problem." They continued by adding, "It is difficult to fail this class…You would have to be consistently late and fail to answer all daily quizzes correctly to fail this course…and no one has failed it the second time." I was incredibly relieved upon hearing that, as anyone with my fear of needles would understand.

I finished a week-long intensive first aid training and went home to my spouse after staying in a hotel during the course. Even though I was excited to complete the course on my first try, 2023 turned out to be a year filled with personal and professional challenges. These challenges not only increased stress while trying to finish everything on time but also significantly influenced my journey. As I started embracing this new chapter, the number of unexpected obstacles that suddenly appeared was astonishing. A month before I received the official notice of my overseas assignment, my spouse and I had to change our international travel plans. We had planned a guided tour of Peru, a country high on our travel bucket list, and one of two places my spouse wanted to visit for his birthday, the other being Australia.

***

We booked the tour through a reputable U.S. travel company, planning to visit iconic sites like Machu Picchu, the Sacred Valley, and Lake Titicaca. However, escalating political unrest in Peru arose, and the quick updates to U.S. travel advisories about traveling elsewhere prompted us to change our plans. Prioritizing safety, we decided to switch our destination to Costa Rica. I can honestly say we made the right choice in changing our plans and taking a guided tour of Costa Rica instead of Peru. Costa Rica offered a striking contrast to the landscapes, wildlife, and environment we are used to in the continental United States. My spouse and I explored lush tropical rainforests, crossed hanging bridges amid the treetops, visited a coffee plantation, and cruised a river, marveling at the wildlife with every stop on the guided tour, spotting crocodiles, monkeys, and exotic birds. The experience was an unforgettable example of the flexibility and adaptability that travel often demands.

Travel quickly became a central part of our relationship. From the beginning, we bonded over our shared love for exploring new places, or as we call it, "seeing the world." Even before the COVID-19 pandemic and the subsequent lockdowns, we committed ourselves to travel, carefully planning both domestic and international trips from 2021 to 2023, focusing on experiences rather than possessions.

As May 2023 approached, we committed to moving forward with our revised plans and guided tour of Costa Rica. Several factors influenced this decision. First, by then, we both knew I would be leaving for my overseas assignment either at the end of 2023 or early 2024—I had not yet received an official departure date. We wanted to share an adventure in an exotic location and cherish the quality time together before I left for four months overseas for work. Second, my spouse was determined to celebrate his birthday abroad. Third, the news that my spouse's mother was diagnosed with cancer made the trip an essential emotional escape.

May was also a month of celebration! My partner accepted the marriage proposal I had hinted at since at least fall 2021. In a charming twist, he also proposed to me. The proposal was not the typical get-down-on-one-knee kind. Instead, it happened during a casual conversation while we were driving down the road. I would say it was one of those moments when the idea suddenly popped into my spouse's head, and the words just slipped right out of his mouth — not surprising, given my spouse. In fact, I enjoy teasing him now and then, reminding him I asked first. Before eloping, my spouse's brother and sister-in-law came for their annual visit. We decided — all four of us together — that instead of sightseeing in Virginia and nearby states, we would take a road trip to Niagara Falls. While my brother-in-law and his wife traveled with us, my spouse and I debated whether to tell them. We chose to wait and keep it a secret, with plans to elope in June.

As June arrived, our elopement plans came together smoothly. We arranged a few casual outings with close friends who felt like family. Keeping our wedding a secret increased the excitement, especially when two of our closest female friends started asking about any plans to get married. January 2023 marked four years together, and these friends knew it! We considered sharing our plan to elope a few times but remained committed to keeping it quiet, supporting each other emotionally to maintain the surprise.

Two weeks before the big day, we decided to elope, and another friend planned an outdoor grilling event. She invited us along with other family and close friends who happened to be visiting the same day we chose to elope. We decided to attend and use the gathering as a subtle way to celebrate our marriage. On the drive over, we thought about how best to reveal our secret. Should we tell them as we walk in the door, or keep quiet and see if they notice? We chose the latter.

We arrived at our friend's house, which was bustling with activity even though it was late, but we had told everyone we would be there. My spouse immediately caught my subtle attempt to see if the friends would notice our wedding rings by deliberately passing items to them with the hand that had a wedding ring on it. As we continued mingling, I grew increasingly impatient because no one was paying attention. I decided to walk over to the kitchen area to talk with the host of the gathering and her sister. The deliberate placement of my hand on the back of the barstool to draw attention to my wedding ring caused my spouse to step back to avoid laughing out loud at my effort.

Finally! One of the friends who asked if we had plans to get married saw my ring, gasped, and exclaimed, "ARE YOU KIDDING ME... ARE YOU F***ING KIDDING ME?!" while grabbing my hand and catching her husband and sister's attention, the latter being the host of the party. Her shouting was a mix of joy and mock annoyance, followed by, "LOOK! The two of them got married!" The supposed annoyance was just her reaction to realizing we had eloped and did not invite anyone. Laughter soon followed, along with tears of happiness streaming down our faces. It was a perfect reaction and a beautiful start to our next chapter together.

As my overseas assignment neared, the growing pressure and stress from paperwork and training, while trying to manage my usual workload, began to take a toll on me. My caring, cheerful Puerto Rican spouse, always attentive to my well-being, reminded me that we had not one, but two relaxing trips planned. The first was a Western Caribbean cruise, and the second was a Christmas getaway to Puerto Rico.

The cruise would offer a much-needed escape to reduce stress caused by increasing paperwork, training, my regular work duties, and the growing concern we both shared about his mother's health as she continued her chemotherapy sessions in her fight against cancer. The second getaway, spending Christmas in my spouse's birthplace of Puerto Rico, carried special significance, providing an opportunity to reconnect with his family and friends and, most importantly, to spend the holiday season with his mom. She was the most important woman in his life.

2

Arrival and the Initial Two-Week Ordeal

On the evening of February 21, 2024, I drove to Dulles International Airport, one of three international airports serving the Washington, D.C., metropolitan area, to catch the first leg of my flight to Amman, Jordan. I was nervous but also eager for time to pass faster so I could board the plane and start my overseas assignment in Jordan. My thinking was that the sooner I arrived, the sooner my assignment would begin, and I could go home again. Unfortunately, the plane I was supposed to board had mechanical issues, causing a delay. I finally boarded the plane just before midnight, heading to Frankfurt, Germany, for a layover that was initially supposed to be eight hours but was shortened to only four and a half hours. The flight from Germany to Jordan went smoothly, and I arrived at Queen Alia International Airport in Amman around 8:00 p.m. local time. I was able to clear customs surprisingly quickly and made my way to the main terminal, where I met my supervisor—the analyst I would be replacing at the facility—and a female teammate who would be with me during the first half of my rotation.

The supervisor suggested I grab something from Starbucks at the airport because, once we left and entered the facility, we were not allowed outside the perimeter walls unless on official travel orders. I grabbed a cup of Spanish Coffee, a sandwich, and brownie bites to go. The team escorted me to the vehicle and started our journey back to the facility. As we drove through the dimly lit streets of Amman, I took in the unfamiliar sights and smells of the city. There was a stinky yet dingy scent in the air that immediately reminded me I was far from home in a foreign country. I found the mosques, all lit up with mint-green exterior lighting, to be interesting. As we moved farther out of the city, the traffic began to decrease, and the scent in the air shifted to one of sand, dirt, and roadside trash.

My teammates quickly filled me in on the current situation and what to expect once we arrived at the facility. They explained that the facility was located in a less desirable area and that it was common to wake up smelling burning trash, sometimes with unknown items being burned. I was also told that if we had the chance to leave the facility, such as for a run in the surrounding desert, we needed to stay alert for the numerous feral dogs roaming around the perimeter, as they could attack if given the opportunity. About 45 minutes later, we reached the facility. The process of getting onto the base was well organized but detailed, ensuring there were no bombs under the vehicle's undercarriage while parked in the airport lot. We then drove through one perimeter checkpoint to another, which led us into the main area of the facility—where I would sleep, play, and work every day for the next four months. Even after three weeks of training, an extra week of first aid training, and roughly eight months' worth of paperwork, I still felt unprepared and unsure of what to expect. Being my first overseas assignment, I had mixed feelings—both determination and nervousness. I felt ready to handle my responsibilities and face any challenges, but I also recognized my limits.

The analyst I would replace at the facility and the supervisor helped me get my luggage out of the vehicle, and I started to head up the stairs into the building that housed my sleeping quarters. The female teammate who rode along to pick me up at the airport directed me to my quarters, saying, "It is at the end of the hall to the left, where you will see your name displayed next to the door at eye level."

After dropping off my luggage, I decided to accept the supervisor's offer to walk over to the chow hall for a late-night meal known as "mid-reps." During dinner, the supervisor, and the analyst I was replacing at the facility gave me some additional practical advice about the food situation. I was told that mid-reps and breakfast were the most reliable, while lunch menus varied from decent to bad, and dinner was unpredictable. It was recommended that on certain days, dining at the café down the road would be a smart choice; it featured pizza and Lebanese cuisine. Jet-lagged and adjusting to an eight-hour time difference, I headed to my room to sleep and prepare for the days ahead.

I woke up around 8:30 a.m. local time on Friday, February 23, 2024, and went to the main operations building to meet my team and start the process of accessing my accounts and other lines of business. Also, I was hungry. When I asked about breakfast, I was told the chow hall is closed and would not reopen until lunch. However, the café down the road was open and still served breakfast. The analyst I was replacing, and I then walked across the base to the café. I was still a bit nervous on my first day and wanted to make a good first impression, while also eager to dive into learning the assignments and tasks that would be delegated to me over the next four months.

It took about fifteen minutes to reach the café. After reviewing the menu, my predecessor kindly helped speed up my decision by pointing out items he could vouch for as excellent. I trusted his judgment and ordered a Nutella-filled toasted pita and a turkey-and-cheese toasted pita. Also, mornings are not complete for me without my cup of coffee. About ten minutes later, my order was ready; I grabbed it to go and headed back across the base for a 10:00 a.m. meeting.

During the walk back with my predecessor, I listened and took in my unfamiliar surroundings at the same time. The skies were clear that morning, with a deep blue hue, a cool breeze, and the sun gradually warming the air. There was a light amount of sand and dirt in the atmosphere, but overall, the outside air felt refreshing. As we continued walking back to the main facility, I began to gain a clearer understanding of my responsibilities. My predecessor explained that I would support two teams. My primary team was in the main operations building we exited this morning on the way to the café. There was another team I would support in a secondary role, as a Data Scientist. This team was in the secondary operations building, across the street from the main building, called the "Data Team," which consisted of data engineers and software developers. As I listened to my predecessor, I found myself thinking, I hope they are not expecting me to be a data engineer or software developer!

We arrived at the secondary operations building for the group meeting about five minutes early. In the data lounge, the entire Data Team was present, including two women and at least six men. The other data scientist from my primary team—referred to here as the "geoscience team"—was already seated. The members of the Data Team were all polite and welcoming. The team leader, a Canadian Army captain, immediately stood out. He quickly stood up and introduced himself. As he approached, I could not help but notice the spark in his eyes, his bashful smile, and his friendly demeanor. He also made sure he was among the first to shake my hand, highlighted his leadership role, and invited me to sit next to him during the meeting. His enthusiasm for having me sit beside him seemed both professional and genuinely warm. Everyone on the Data Team made a good first impression, although no one appeared as energetic that day as the team leader.

As each member of the Data Team introduced themselves, they shared both professional and personal details. When it was my turn, before I could say anything, one of the two women on the team showed interest in whether my wife supported my four-month overseas assignment. I decided to be honest and correct their assumption that my spouse was not female, but that I was married to a man. I quickly explained, "I want to be honest because it would likely slip out that my spouse is a man, and I do not want to make anyone feel awkward suddenly." I continued by saying, "I understand if that makes anyone uncomfortable." Their reactions appeared positive, as both women assured me that everyone on the team is accepting and comfortable. For now, I felt a sense of relief.

The first day involved setting up accounts and onboarding. As I moved back and forth between buildings with my predecessor to get necessary accounts created and equipment acquired, the Canadian captain's constant attentiveness quickly made us uncomfortable. I could not tell at the time whether he was flirting or just annoyingly friendly. Each time we crossed paths, he greeted me with a smile, showed strong enthusiasm, and promptly asked Data Team woman #1 if the desk next to him was vacant.

She replied, "No," but motioned toward the empty desks. The captain insisted that I select the desk closest to him, saying, "He will assist me with anything I need." Woman #1 of the Data Team immediately said, "She will get my workstation ready as soon as possible," while glancing somewhat annoyed at the Canadian captain, trying to boost his leadership status as team lead of the Data Team.

Until my accounts were fully established, my predecessor stated, "You will work exclusively out of the primary operations building." I was relieved knowing I would be physically separated from the Canadian captain. This separation allowed me to engage with my primary team and focus on my assigned projects without distractions from a man whose persistent attention had quickly become both uncomfortable and annoying. However, his presence remained constant. The captain would make deliberate trips to the main operations building to gaze at me from across the room, gain my attention by calling out my name, and then grin ear to ear when I looked up.

The captain's actions throughout the day were unacceptable. Three times, I felt a creepy vibe wash over me, telling me I was being watched. I would look up, and he would be staring at me intently. The situation quickly became troubling because his main workstation was in the secondary operations building, but he was in the primary operations building observing me from a distance. At that moment, I could not tell if I had said something that made him think I was interested in him. It was my first day at the facility, and this captain seemed to be flirting with me! I started wondering: Should I say something? Maybe just ignore his behavior? I might be overreacting.

His actions on my first day drew the attention of several people. A few asked who he was. I told them he was the team leader for the Data Team. He worked in the secondary operations building but was also part of the Canadian team. These people, also from the U.S., simply nodded to confirm that this person was not bothering me. Even though I was concerned about his actions on my first day, I did not want to cause any trouble. I decided it was best to ignore his overt attempts to get my attention, as much as I could, and dismiss them as him just trying to be friendly.

Saturday, February 24, passed quickly. Although most foreign representatives had permission to leave the facility for the weekend, Americans had to stay on-site due to regional instability. The ongoing Israel–Hamas conflict, along with heightened tensions in Yemen, Syria, and Iran, led military leaders to consider Jordan unsafe for both U.S. military and civilian personnel to venture outside the facility unless on official duty. Israel's strong military stance further supported our decision to remain. Even though I was confined to the facility, I participated in activities suggested by my team leader to boost morale. To my surprise, the day brought a pleasant sense of relief. I genuinely felt relaxed as the hours passed. For a while, I almost forgot about the Canadian captain and his overly friendly attitude, but then Sunday arrived.

On February 25, the foreign representatives, who were also housed inside the facility, gradually started returning to the base. The captain resumed his usual routine, often appearing in the main operations building. In fact, that Sunday, he seemed to arrive earlier than his fellow Canadians. When he saw me, his face showed an unsettling expression, as if he was eager to see me. He called my name repeatedly and kept watching me from across the room. Later that afternoon, everyone from the main operations building went across the street to the secondary operations building for the weekly stand-up.

The weekly stand-up was a routine briefing on upcoming work and training activities at the facility. During the briefing, I started feeling like I was being watched. I looked across the room, and the Canadian captain was staring directly at me. Each time our eyes met, he puffed out his chest and smiled proudly. Most of his Canadian colleagues already knew who I was, even though I had yet to learn their names. It was only my third day onsite.

About an hour after the stand-up, he returned to the main building. He came around the corner and loudly called out my name, catching my attention, just as he did on Friday, to announce his presence. He continued smiling in my direction while chatting with his teammates. A few of the other Canadians started smiling and looking my way as well. What the captain had told them remains unknown, but their ability to recognize me by name and sight said a lot. I decided to lower my standing desk and sit in the chair to avoid further distractions, ignore the captain's unsettling behavior, and focus on my work. My tasks included supporting teammates with Python, SQL, and JSON scripting to compile data for a customer-facing map application. By Sunday evening, I felt exhausted both mentally and emotionally, but also satisfied that I had maintained focus and progress in my duties.

The next morning, Monday, February 26th, the captain was waiting and watching for me to come out of my quarters. As I walked down the stairs and onto the street toward the main operations building, he exited his dormitory and fell into step beside me. He greeted me with a smile after calling out my name to get my attention, offering shy eye contact but eager to talk. During the walk, he touched my arm, shoulder, and back, asked how I was doing, and reiterated his willingness to help. He mentioned his planned departure in late March and expressed regret that we would not have much more time together, implying he wished that were not the case. Again, he stated his willingness to assist and wanted to help me with anything. Although it only took a few minutes to walk from the sleeping quarters to the main operations building, it somehow felt longer. When I reached the walkway to enter the main building, he said with a smile, "See you later," in an awkward, flirtatious way before heading toward the secondary operations building.

He continued to appear in the main operations building throughout the day, often watching me from across the room on the work floor, where all the other Canadians sat. I would see the captain position himself in the doorway of the Canadians' conference room or sit inside with his feet up on the desk, the door wide open and angled so he had a clear line of sight to me. While I tried to stay focused on my work, I could not help but wonder: How could you be more obvious that you are flirting with me? Later that evening, he sat in the Oasis—a green space in front of the main operations building entrance—calling out my name when he saw me passing by.

I tried to ignore it but quickly realized I could not. He visibly became agitated, and since I was on a base surrounded by military personnel, including enlisted members and officers from multiple foreign countries, with nowhere to go, I did not want any trouble. When he stood up and started to approach me, I quickly pretended I was zoning out and apologized for my delayed reply. He asked where I was headed, and I said I was going to work out. While at the gym and in the middle of my workout, I suddenly felt watched. I looked into the mirror and saw him, still in full uniform, staring intently at me while I trained. He quickly started a conversation with someone else he knew, grabbing water from the cooler at the same time. Each building had its own water cooler, so his presence at the gym could not have been a coincidence.

On Tuesday, February 27, the captain's behavior became more intense. He immediately approached me, placed his hand on my shoulder, and then moved it down to my back. He complimented my appearance, saying, "You look nice today…The outfit you are wearing looks good on you…t shows your muscle tone nicely." In that moment, I trusted my gut instinct that I had been telling myself to ignore—that the Canadian captain was flirting and sexually attracted to me. My discomfort quickly grew.

I tried to avoid the captain for the rest of the day. Unfortunately, while working out, I caught him staring at me again. This time, he tried to hide his reason for being at the gym by interrupting another Canadian who was working out to ask work-related questions. That night, I went for a walk in the cool air to clear my head, hoping I would not run into the captain I had been dodging all day. As I made my way down the road back to my sleeping quarters, he emerged from the darkness near a bunker between the sleeping quarters.

He called out my name and asked if I wanted to go somewhere private with him, specifically the bunker against which he was standing. I responded cautiously, "Why? I did not hear any alerts or notifications about a drill or real threat."

He laughed, replying, "No, no drill—I just thought you might want to hang out in the bunker with me."

I declined immediately, trying to hide my discomfort by saying, "If that is the case, no, but thank you for asking."

He looked a bit disappointed and seemed embarrassed as he said, "Okay, have a good night," while I walked back to my sleeping quarters to turn in for the night.

The next day, Wednesday, February 28, he looked disappointed when he saw me but still greeted me with, "Hi, [my name]." I responded politely, using his first name to keep things professional, which eased his attitude. Although I had turned down his invitation the night before, I wanted to show I was open to maintaining a professional relationship. He approached me less often that day. The Data Team, along with his fellow Canadian military personnel on the base, was very talkative that day. They all kept praising the captain while glancing in my direction or directly addressing me.

The day ended with my team leader announcing that we would have a pizza party with the Data Team. The other data scientist on my team mentioned that the captain and team leader believed the event would help foster better engagement between the teams. I did not mind having pizza and thought it would be a great way to take a break from work. However, I could not shake the feeling that the captain's enthusiasm for the pizza party, the constant praise about the captain from the Data Team, and the unusual comment made by the other data scientist on my team made me suspect there might be more to the pizza party than just innocent team building.

Thinking that my declined request to enter the bunker with the caption had worked, based on his decreased engagement on Wednesday, I had hoped this change would become the new norm moving forward. I was wrong. The next day, February 29, 2024, I attended the group pizza party organized by the leaders of both my primary team and the Data Team. While the event celebrated ongoing collaboration, it quickly became clear that the captain had orchestrated the gathering as a subtle attempt to get closer to me under the pretense of team bonding.

Several team members started to emphasize their earlier comments about how impressive the Canadian captain was and how I should interact with him. These comments included, but was not limited to, "The captain has taken a liking to you," and "He's been paying a lot of attention to you since your arrival." Meanwhile, Female Data Team member #1 mentioned, "The captain is running late but will be here soon," while deliberately looking directly at me. Her remark only made things more awkward, as it immediately caused several people to glance toward me. Two members of the Data Team quickly discussed how interesting it was that many people sent here for overseas assignments often get involved sexually outside of work. Without hesitation, I firmly said, "I am here solely to work," which clearly unsettled some of the attendees.

This uncomfortable banter lasted about ten minutes before it ended as the captain entered the room. He stood in the doorway, looking directly at me. After a few minutes of this, a teammate from the Data Team asked him whether he was going to sit down or just stand there all night. Clearly embarrassed, he moved to the nearest available seat—conspicuously not next to me—despite playful teasing from at least two teammates: "You're not going to sit by [my name]?" His evasive reply, "Maybe later," prompted a sarcastic comment from another: "Good, maybe you'll finally start paying attention to us instead of giving all your attention to [my name]." Though meant as a joke, such comments, repeated over the past two days by his teammates and others from his home country, had already unsettled me. Even from across the room, he positioned himself to keep me within his line of sight.

The pizza was quickly set out for people to grab a slice despite the mounting tension and sarcastic remarks. I stood up to get a slice, hoping to lighten the mood. Almost immediately, the captain also stood and moved to the now-empty seat beside me, maintaining steady eye contact. To shift the focus, I engaged others across the room in conversation, but within fifteen minutes, I was talking with the captain again. He asked if I had ever been to Canada and if I liked it. I shared that Montreal and Ottawa were my favorite cities among the four I had visited. He quickly followed up by asking if I would consider moving to Ottawa, adding, "That's where I live... we could get together." Pleased with the exchange, he enthusiastically agreed with my positive remarks about Canada.

I mentioned my admiration for the Canadian Mounted Police uniforms, noting how cool I thought they looked. He responded eagerly, sharing that he had considered joining the Mounted Police before opting for the army. When he pressed me again about moving to Ottawa to be close to him, the question struck me as unusual. Several colleagues from both teams looked equally surprised; although no one spoke aloud, their body language revealed their discomfort. I maintained my composure, casually explaining that I loved living in the Washington, D.C., area, emphasizing that my family, friends, and career were there, and I would not trade that for anything. The conversation then shifted to his twin sister, who also lived in Ottawa and, he said, might like me if we met. He spoke fondly of living in Ottawa, despite his family's origins in France and their settlement near Montreal, Quebec.

After about thirty minutes of one-on-one discussion, he excused himself, citing unfinished work before the end of his day.

Less than twenty minutes later, the gathering dispersed. The pizza party was held in the foreign representatives' building, colloquially called the "Frat House," which had lounges for each country on the base, along with a lounge specifically for the Data Team. We cleaned the room together, secured it, and left before the 10:00 p.m. curfew. Several facility members warned me that inappropriate activities, including physical fights and sexual misconduct, sometimes occurred in the Frat House, often fueled by overindulgence in the recreational lounges meant for relaxation.

I returned to the main operations building to wrap up my day. By then, it was past 8:00 p.m. As I climbed the stairs, I saw the captain leaving the secondary operations building. As usual, he spotted me across the street, called my name cheerfully, and grinned widely upon seeing me.

The next morning, March 1, 2024, I saw the captain again. He touched my arm—a bold move in front of a senior Canadian officer. About fifteen minutes later, we crossed paths somewhere else in the facility, where he looked visibly embarrassed. I guessed he had been reprimanded for his earlier behavior. After that, he changed his approach noticeably. He kept more physical distance but still watched me from afar, often spending time in the Oasis area with different Canadian teammates—sometimes alone, sometimes in groups. Every time we met, he greeted me by name.

I also noticed that several Canadians who arrived with him became more attentive to my movements throughout the day. It was unsettling to realize that no matter where I went on the compound, the captain would show up within ten to fifteen minutes—either walking nearby or starting a conversation.

Determined to avoid more unwanted attention, I chose to work out in a different part of the facility that day. During my session, I saw the captain and his teammates lifting weights and running nearby. Later, one of them—whom I will call Canadian #1—entered the gym shortly after me, briefly went into the locker room, and left within three minutes, walking past me while texting. His behavior felt invasive and unsettling.

After finishing my workout and having lunch, I noticed another Canadian, Canadian #2, sitting alone. To stay professional while keeping my distance from the captain, I took a seat across from Canadian #2 and started a casual conversation. At first, Canadian #1 approached and sat nearby, clearly uneasy with my deliberate engagement with Canadian #2. However, he eventually joined the talk. After about thirty minutes, I excused myself, feeling I had left a good impression.

On March 2, the facility seemed noticeably quieter, and for the first time in days, I felt a sense of safety. It was a Saturday, and as usual, foreign representatives were allowed to leave the compound. Unfortunately, the captain's intrusive behavior resumed the next day. During the weekly stand-up on March 3, all three Canadians, along with a fourth—whom I will call Canadian #3—stood together across from me, watching closely. Throughout the day, they repeatedly looked for opportunities to greet me. The captain resumed his unwelcome advances, touching my arm and back while commenting on my increasingly muscular and toned appearance.

On March 4, I intentionally chose to work out at the outdoor gym on the main street, fully aware that the captain and the other three Canadians often spent time there. My goal was to increase my visibility and hopefully discourage any extended surveillance. During my session, I saw the captain, Canadian #1, and Canadian #2 in various nearby spots—lifting weights and running.

Later that afternoon, the captain asked for my personal cell number so he could add me to the Data Team group chat. Unsure how to respond, I gave him my personal contact, and he promptly added me. The following day, realizing my mistake, I corrected it by providing my work number to prevent further intrusion.

That same day, determined to maintain boundaries, I chose to ignore the captain despite expecting tension. During lunch, he loudly tried to get my attention, drawing curious glances from officers of other nations. After waiting at least ten minutes without engaging, I left the cafeteria, assuming he had left. To my surprise, he and Canadian #1 stood between access points, glaring at me from a distance. As I approached within fifty feet, the captain turned to Canadian #1 and said, "Let's go," and they walked ahead into their dormitory, located directly across from mine. I could not help but notice the captain's side glance and the visible frustration on his face as he closed the door behind them—obvious signs that he knew I was nearby.

Back in my quarters, I discovered a private message from the captain on my work phone, sent shortly after he added me to the group chat. Though hesitant to respond given my efforts to avoid him, I eventually replied. About an hour later, he appeared, visibly pleased by my response.

That night, I was haunted by a vivid nightmare in which the captain and his teammates broke into my quarters or lured me into a bunker. I reminded myself it was only a dream and tried to shake off the unease before returning to sleep.

On March 6, following a demonstration led by Team Sweden, I remained behind to engage in discussions about data science. During this time, I overheard members of the Data Team remarking that the surveillance cameras did not cover the bunkers, which they noted were frequently used for sexual encounters. I responded by emphasizing that I was there solely to work. In that moment, I finally grasped the true implications behind the captain's earlier suggestion to accompany him to the bunker.

On March 7, I remained focused on my assignments despite the ongoing unwanted attention from the captain. That week, I met the new sergeant, who emphasized her approachability and openness, providing a small measure of reassurance amid the tension. I continued to maintain professionalism and deliberately chose to ignore the captain's behavior.

That night, I woke up from a vivid and deeply disturbing nightmare. In the dream, the captain grabbed me from behind while Canadian #1, Canadian #2, and two unidentified people held my arms and legs. I tried to break free, but their aggression grew worse. The dream then shifted to an out-of-body view, where I saw myself being kicked and bones breaking. Amidst the chaos, I heard the captain's voice commanding silence and telling them to drag me into a bunker. Just as my head and arms sank into the darkness, I jolted awake, sweating, shaken, and desperately trying to tell myself it was only a nightmare. Still, the fear remained.

On March 8, I decided to work out outdoors at what we called Jersey Shore along the main street to stay visible. While I exercised, I saw the captain entering the secondary operations building with a man in a gray business suit. Wearing sunglasses, he kept steady eye contact with me as he climbed the stairs, clearly indicating I was under his watchful gaze. About twenty minutes into my workout, I felt an intense sensation of being watched. I tried to tell myself it was just my imagination—after all, the captain seemed busy with a meeting with the visiting official. Still, the feeling lingered.

Scanning my surroundings, I saw no one in my immediate line of sight or peripheral vision. Then, a voice in my mind urged me to look behind me. When I did, I caught Canadian #2 watching me. The expression on his face is etched in my memory: unmistakable lust and intent, conveyed through his eyes, posture, and every subtle gesture. It was an unmistakable, chilling confirmation of his intentions.

Fear surged through me—raw, undeniable fear—the kind that signaled real danger. His reaction was immediate; he startled, and a flicker of panic crossed his eyes when he realized I had caught him. Quickly averting his gaze, he pulled out his phone, pretending to text as he slowly moved back toward the main operations building. I could almost hear his thoughts: *He caught me looking. I need to act natural.*

As he walked away, he glanced furtively over his shoulder, trying to see if I was still watching. I was, though I wished I were not. I struggled to reconcile what I had just witnessed.

In that moment, a chilling realization settled over me: The captain might be conspiring with his Canadian teammates. My disturbing nightmares were not mere dreams but premonitions. Countless troubling thoughts swirled through my mind.

I could not decide who unsettled me more—the captain, who openly flirted with me while displaying possessiveness and anger, or Canadian #2, whose look revealed a darker intent before he noticed my awareness. I feared them both.

Determined to continue, I resolved to finish my workout and seek support from the sergeant I had met the day before.

3

Fear, Doubt, and Disclosure

After finishing my workout, I headed toward the main operations building, hoping to find the new sergeant. Although the building was just across the street and one block over from the outdoor gym, it felt painfully distant. I could not shake the image of Canadian #2 watching me earlier, his expression heavy with lust, his body language unmistakable. Every instinct urged me to speak with the sergeant, a leader who had made it clear she welcomed both personal and official concerns.

As I walked, I struggled with how to frame the conversation. Should I approach it as a personal issue or present it officially? The closer I got to the entrance, the more uneasy I felt. What if Canadian #2 was already inside? I had seen him heading that way after I caught him staring. What if the Canadian captain—whom I saw earlier entering the secondary operations building—had returned? What if I ran into all three Canadians? What if I could not even find the sergeant? I debated how to ask for her time: Should I request a personal meeting or keep it official? And if I made it official, how would my team lead respond? I kept thinking, I do not want any trouble. Would they even believe me?

I badge into the building and, without thinking, head straight to the leadership section. A fellow officer told me the sergeant was in a meeting but expected to be back soon. The thought of staying inside the main operations building only worsened my growing fears. Anxiety clenched my chest, and I could feel the early signs of a panic attack coming on. I turned to leave.

As I approached the exit, the sergeant walked through the doorway. I stopped her and asked if she had a moment. I assured her it was not an emergency, just something I needed to share with her. I reminded her of the offer she had made, that we could come to her with anything. She paused, then replied, "I am still in the middle of something, but I will be available in about 30 minutes. Can you wait?" I told her I could.

Outside again, I stayed on edge. The panic had not gone away; I just masked it as best I could. Still, my effort to hide it was failing—at least five people, including the sergeant, who had already asked if I was okay. I headed to my quarters to collect myself. Just as I reached the door, the alarms sounded—a scheduled bunker drill. It suddenly made sense why the sergeant had said she was tied up. I rushed into the nearest bunker beside my dorm, but my fear was not about the simulation of a missile threat. It was the thought that one of the Canadians—especially the captain and Canadians #1, #2, and #3—might enter the same enclosed space. That possibility made me nauseous. I counted the minutes until the drill ended.

When the all-clear sounded, I returned to the main operations building for roll call. Afterward, my team leader approached and immediately asked if I was all right. I told him I was going to shower—something I had intended to do after my workout—and then meet with the new sergeant. He asked if he needed to be present. I told him no; the meeting was not at an official capacity.

After the all-clear, I left the main operations building and returned to my quarters. Once inside, I took a deep breath and stepped into the shower, hoping to clear my mind. As the water ran over me, I struggled with whether I should talk to the sergeant about what had happened just an hour earlier. Should I tell her everything from the start? Should I present it as a misunderstanding, something I thought was suspicious but meant nothing? Would she listen, or would she cut me off mid-sentence and accuse me of overreacting?

The internal conflict overwhelmed me. My anxiety surged, turning into a toxic mix of self-doubt and self-blame. I started to wonder if I had somehow caused everything. Did I say something, or unknowingly give off signals through my body language that encouraged the Canadian captain's advances? Self-reflection quickly took over. I replayed every interaction since I arrived, searching for signs I missed or mistakes I had made.

Thoughts raced through my mind like a fighter jet at Mach 3. I finished my shower, got dressed, and prepared to head back to the main operations building. As I stepped outside, I told myself to stop overthinking and just talk to the sergeant. She had emphasized her approachability and made it clear that personal concerns were welcome. At worst, she might say I was overreacting, but something inside me insisted I speak up anyway. I needed her advice, and I needed to know how best to move forward.

As I entered the main operations building, I made a direct line toward the leadership area. Instead of taking the main walkway, which would have taken me past the Canadian representatives' footprint, I chose a less conspicuous route through the back. I hoped to find the sergeant and see if she was available to talk. Fortunately, she spotted me before I even reached her workstation. She immediately noticed my anxious expression and suggested we take a walk around the complex rather than talk inside an office or meeting room. I welcomed the idea. The thought of walking outdoors felt far more comfortable—and far less intimidating—than sitting in a closed space surrounded by the typical, sterile white walls of a government building.

We exited the main operations building and began walking down the stairs when the sergeant quickly suggested we put some distance between ourselves and the entrance before starting the conversation. As we passed the oasis and restroom building and made our way onto the road leading toward the dorms, my heart pounded with anxiety. I feared not being believed, or, worse, being seen by the very individuals I was about to report for inappropriate behavior.

The sergeant could sense my unease and offered reassurance. "Relax as we walk," she said. "No one will be listening in. If anyone gets too close, I will tell them to leave. This is a private conversation. Start from the beginning, or wherever you feel most comfortable." I nodded, took a deep breath, and began.

I had barely gotten three sentences out when the Canadian captain, along with Canadian #1, Canadian #3, and several others, suddenly poured out of the buildings for a military fitness run. The captain, upon seeing me walking beside the sergeant, visibly stumbled over nothing. Every instinct in me wanted to point him out at once; to say, *That is the man I'm talking about.* But I held back. Speaking up in that moment would have drawn immediate attention and undermined any chance of filing an anonymous report—if that is what I decided to do, depending on the sergeant's guidance.

We kept walking as the captain and others ran past us. I picked up where I left off, recalling my first day on the platform and the captain's unusually intense focus. When I said that Saturdays were the only days I felt safe—because I knew the captain was off-site—the sergeant's face instantly changed, showing concern. Her reaction, along with her attentive stance and focused look, told me she was listening, understanding, and most importantly, believing me. That belief, in that moment, meant everything. The tension in my body started to ease.

It took us about two full laps around the complex for me to share everything. I tried to be concise but thorough, focusing on the details I believed really mattered. When I finally indicated I was done, the sergeant took a deep breath before replying. She started by telling me I was brave for coming forward. I did not feel brave—just embarrassed, foolish, and ashamed that I had somehow ended up in this situation. Still, I stayed silent and listened. She suggested I consider talking with the on-site chaplain, the psychologist, or both, and urged me to make sure my team leader was informed sooner rather than later. She made it clear that the decision was entirely mine and assured me she would not—and could not—force anything. But she encouraged me to seriously think about the support they could offer.

After our conversation, I decided to get dinner at the cafeteria. While I was eating, I noticed Canadian #1 sitting alone and unusually close, watching me intently. It struck me as odd—this was the first time I had seen a Canadian representative sitting alone. If he hoped to overhear a conversation or expected an invitation to join me, he was going to be disappointed. Talking about my earlier discussion with the sergeant was the last thing on my mind.

I finished dinner and returned to the main operations building to wrap up the rest of the day. Conversations across the floor buzzed with excitement: it was Friday, the only day when personnel could enjoy two alcoholic drinks. As the chatter swirled around me, I reflected on everything that had happened. After such a mentally and emotionally draining day, I started to think it might be best to spend the evening quietly in my quarters. Just as I was debating whether to skip the Friday social, the sergeant and her commanding officer walked by. The sergeant made a point to say she expected us all to attend the event and looked directly at me as she said it. I told her I would stop by for a little while, but did not plan to stay long. I was exhausted.

Before I left the building, I ran into the sergeant...again. She quietly pulled me aside and said she would understand if I decided not to attend, but added that showing up, even briefly, might help take my mind off everything that had happened. I appreciated her thoughtfulness and decided to go. However, I made a deliberate point to arrive at least 30 minutes into the event.

As I stepped out of the dormitory onto the road leading straight to the social event, a wave of fear and apprehension swept over me, causing the hair on the back of my neck to stand up. I quietly prayed that I would not run into the Canadians who had unsettled me earlier — not outside the dorm and not anywhere along the street. With each step, I realized I was holding my breath, only exhaling when I felt safe. A lingering suspicion told me that at least two of them might intentionally position themselves along the route to watch my reaction.

When I arrived at the event, which was already in progress, I slipped inside the building where drinks were being served. Seeing the sergeant behind the bar immediately put me at ease. Her presence gave me a reassuring feeling of safety. To my surprise, the only attendees I noticed were fellow Americans. This struck me as unusual because these Friday socials usually attracted a small crowd of international guests—Australians, New Zealanders, Britons, and others.

At the Friday social event—where only Americans were present—I immediately became suspicious that people were already talking. It felt like only a matter of time before everyone's fingers would, without a doubt, point in my direction. I cannot begin to express how deeply I feared being seen as the problem or facing retaliation for speaking up about what my instincts told me was serious trouble. The Canadian captain either had an intense, inappropriate fixation on me or harbored a dangerous level of homophobia, both of which sent warning signs that bordered on violence, even fatality. Luckily, around the time I confided in the sergeant, I also told the female teammate who had helped pick me up from the airport the night I arrived. She happened to be at the social and insisted I join her at the football field to play an unusual game others were playing across the street.

The game being played across the street was called Kubb, a Swedish lawn game. The female teammate and others who had sensed earlier today that something was bothering me encouraged me to play. The objective is to use a wooden baton to knock over a row of wooden blocks arranged in front of the opposing team. There are usually five or six blocks lined up about a foot apart. The first team to knock down all the opponent's blocks—and then successfully topple a larger wooden block in the center of the field—wins the game.

Still feeling upset, I drank both of my allotted alcoholic beverages too quickly and found myself slightly tipsy. In that foggy moment, I thought about how my spouse always warned me: "You drink too fast—it always hits you harder." The alcohol did not distract me for long. My mind drifted back to the events of the day. The self-blame crept in again, and I began to replay everything as I started to convince myself I was somehow at fault.

I decided to leave about thirty minutes before the event concluded. Once I returned to my quarters, my team leader, who shared the dorm suite with me, asked for at least the third time that day if I was okay. I told him yes, but in my tipsy, emotional state, I finally opened. I shared everything that had happened that day, along with all the discomfort I had been experiencing since my arrival at the facility.

The concern on his face was unmistakable. He strongly urged me to report the situation and to follow the sergeant's advice by talking to the chaplain or the psychologist, or both. I was emotionally overwhelmed that night. I cried in front of him, and later, I called a close friend. This was the same friend I had previously mentioned regarding the Canadian captain's overly friendly behavior—flirting, touching, and clear boundary violations. When I called, he feared the worst and immediately asked if I had been sexually assaulted. I assured him I did not but went on to describe everything that had happened.

Like the sergeant and my team leader, my friend encouraged me to report the Canadian captain's behavior—that was not only for my own well-being but also for others who might have been affected yet were too afraid to speak out due to fear of retaliation. He believed this might not have been the captain's first time acting inappropriately, but I could be the first willing to come forward. Hearing the same advice from three different people—none of whom knew each other—finally struck a chord. That night, I made a promise to myself: I would talk to the chaplain and seriously consider making an appointment with a psychologist.

I went to bed, but despite knowing the next day was Saturday, a day I had come to appreciate because no foreign representatives would be around, I struggled to fall asleep. Restlessness lingered throughout the night. The next morning, I followed my usual routine with one small exception: I sent emails to both the chaplain and the psychologist. I recalled my team leader's reminder from the night before not to expect a reply until Sunday, given the weekend schedule.

Eager to speak with someone, I took the initiative and went to the on-site chapel just down the road from the cafeteria. After a lengthy conversation with the head chaplain, I learned he could not assist me. The base's religious services were divided into two sectors, and unfortunately, he was responsible for the opposite side. The chaplain assigned to my section was the one I needed to talk to. A mix of embarrassment and disappointment washed over me, but I stayed focused on my duties. I remained hopeful that I could speak with the right chaplain the next day.

The rest of Saturday moved slowly. I found myself anxiously waiting for Sunday, silently hoping the chaplain and psychologist would respond just as my team leader had promised. On Sunday, March 10, 2024, I got up, went through my usual morning routine, and went to work. I had a feeling the chaplain would not respond until after the Sunday stand-up, which usually took place in the afternoon. Sure enough, just as my team leader had said, the chaplain did not reply until after the stand-up.

During the stand-up, the Canadian captain seemed to sense that something was going on. Leading up to the meeting, he repeatedly walked past me—always within ten feet—clearly trying to provoke a reaction. During the meeting itself, instead of standing with the other Canadian representatives, he positioned himself in the area where members from another foreign delegation typically worked. This placement ensured that I had no choice but to walk directly past him. It was obvious he did this intentionally.

The anxiety he triggered in me became overwhelming, and I suddenly felt the urgent need to use the restroom. I hesitated, not wanting to leave the area while he was still nearby. Thankfully, I managed to stall by chatting with a few Americans stationed in the secondary operations building. Eventually, someone from the Data Team came to pull the captain away for something more important than his attempts to intimidate me.

As soon as he left, I made a beeline for the restroom facilities located in a separate building next to the secondary operations center. Just as I approached, I saw the sergeant I had previously confided in exit the women's restroom. I quickly asked her if she would stand watch, explaining that the captain had been deliberately trying to intimidate me. Without hesitation, she agreed, saying, "I'll be here."

Afterward, we returned together to the secondary operations building. Once inside, the sergeant asked if I could discreetly point out the captain, explaining that she had not yet seen what he looked like. I told her he was standing directly to her right but was intentionally hiding his face behind his standing desk—trying to avoid being identified. She tried to glance in his direction without drawing attention but could not get a clear view.

I then asked if she could walk me to the meeting space where the Data Team held their post-stand-up session with the data scientists, engineers, and software developers. She agreed. When we arrived and saw at least three team members already in the room, she quietly returned to the main operations building.

It felt like an eternity before the rest of the team arrived, especially the Canadian captain, who led the group. Ten minutes past the usual start time, one of the team members went to find him. When he finally showed up, he lingered in the doorway, staring directly at me. His tense posture and expression conveyed a strange blend of fear and anger. His change in demeanor was so stark that one of his teammates called him out, saying, "Are you going to come in and sit down, or stand in the doorway looking creepy?" The remark broke the tension just enough to get him moving. He walked in and sat down in his usual seat at the conference table.

The entire meeting was painfully awkward. The tension was palpable, made worse by at least three team members asking if the captain was all right. Each time, he claimed he was only tired from a fun Saturday night spent off-site with his fellow Canadians. Still, he avoided looking in my direction for fear of making direct eye contact with me. I could feel suspicion growing in the room. The glances exchanged among the team and the captain's erratic behavior only intensified my anxiety. It felt inevitable that they would soon piece everything together and shift their focus toward me.

The meeting lasted approximately forty-five minutes. The moment it ended, I hurried out of the room. The captain followed closely, clearly intent on stopping or confronting me. I did not wait to find out which. I pushed through the main entrance of the secondary operations building and made a direct line across the street to the main operations building. Once inside and seated at my desk, I finally exhaled and took a deep breath.

I logged in to my computer and checked for any messages from the chaplain or the psychologist. Among several unread emails, one stood out—it was from the chaplain. He noted that he would be available after the Sunday stand-up in the secondary operations building and would remain so until 4:00 p.m. My stomach dropped. The same building I had just fled was where I now had to return.

Reluctantly, I locked my computer and stepped back outside. As I crossed the street toward the secondary operations building, I saw the captain exiting and walking straight toward me. Even from a distance, I could tell he recognized me—and he did not slow his pace. I debated whether to change direction when I noticed another member of the Data Team—let us call him Data Team Member #1. A young, charismatic data engineer from the Washington, D.C., area, he was known for his high-energy storytelling. No matter the topic, his animated delivery always drew people in.

Seeing him gave me an immediate excuse to go over. I quickly approached him, pretending to follow up on a comment he made during the post-stand-up meeting. We stopped near the small building that housed the restrooms, about fifty yards from the main entrance of the operations building. As we talked, another colleague—the other data scientist on my team—joined us from the opposite direction. The three of us started chatting. Mid-conversation, Data Team Member #1 saw the captain walking toward the main building. The captain kept his eyes averted, clearly avoiding eye contact with me. Just as he reached the stairs, Data Team Member #1 called out loudly to him about a shared project. The captain froze and gave a curt reply: he said he was in the middle of something.

I kept my eyes fixed on my teammates, refusing to acknowledge him directly. From the corner of my eye, I saw him make a sharp turn and head straight toward us. He swerved at the last minute and passed behind me, so close his body nearly brushed against mine. Every muscle in my body tensed. It felt like he might grab me. I could sense his hand graze the space just above the small of my back. Then, without stopping, he slipped into the men's restroom. As he made it inside the door frame of the restroom, he turned and tossed out a bizarre remark: "There are some fine-looking dressed men out here." The comment was calculated, a final attempt to provoke me after failing to elicit a reaction with his physical proximity.

I looked at my colleagues, offered a quick excuse about needing to get to a scheduled meeting, and promised to continue our work conversation later. As I turned to leave, I noticed the captain watching me, visibly confused by my lack of acknowledgment. I did not break stride. I headed back to the secondary operations building to speak with the chaplain.

I stepped into the secondary operations building and made my way to the second floor to meet with the chaplain. My heart was pounding. Just as I had done with the sergeant two days earlier, I carefully recounted the Canadian captain's inappropriate remarks and the unwelcome physical contact that had begun the moment I arrived for my overseas assignment. Speaking the words aloud triggered a fresh wave of anxiety.

I explained that, at first, I thought the captain's behavior was too friendly, a bit much for someone with my reserved personality. However, his actions quickly grew more intense. He started making personalized comments about how I looked in my clothes, praising my muscle tone and admiration for my athleticism—especially since I was just a civilian. His attention started to feel increasingly unsettling. He would stare at me from across the room for extended periods, sometimes holding his gaze for ten to twenty minutes, and he always announced when he arrived and left in a way that made sure I noticed.

Physical contact soon followed. Although he had not touched any private areas, his hands started to linger and drift uncomfortably close during brief encounters. Within days, I noticed troubling signs that others might be involved. At least two to three other Canadian personnel were watching me with unsettling focus, their behavior suggesting something more deliberate, almost calculated. As I shared these details with the chaplain, my voice began to tremble. Emotion built in my chest, especially as I admitted the self-doubt that had taken root. I kept asking myself what I might have said or done to give him—or any of his colleagues—the impression that this kind of attention was welcome.

When I finished speaking, the chaplain sat in thoughtful silence before finally responding. "Wow," he said, "this is an incredibly detailed account." For a moment, I questioned whether he believed me. But then he continued, "I am truly sorry this has happened to you. I believe you—and it never should have happened." A feeling of relief washed over me, hearing him say he believed me. He went on to say that, in his view, I was being actively preyed upon.

Then he asked, "Why did you not come forward sooner?" I explained that I initially assumed the Canadian captain was overly friendly, and I was overreacting. I also mentioned that he had told me he would be leaving the facility at the end of March—just two weeks away. The chaplain did not hesitate. "Given the level of detail you've provided, and everything you've experienced, I believe you're in real danger," he said firmly. "I do not think you have two weeks. It sounds like the captain is escalating his behavior precisely because he knows his time here is running out. And from what you have described, he has chosen you as his final target before he leaves."

The chaplain concluded our conversation by reassuring me that he was not trying to frighten me, but he wanted me to grasp the seriousness of the situation. Drawing on his military experience, he explained that he had seen similar circumstances escalate with devastating outcomes. He then asked if I would be willing to share the name of the person who referred me to him. I told him it was the new sergeant who had arrived at the facility earlier that week. When he confirmed her name, I nodded.

He asked if I was comfortable with the sergeant joining us. I told him I did not mind. He called her immediately, and to my surprise, she was at her desk and agreed to come over. While we waited, the chaplain asked me two questions. The first was whether I would be comfortable identifying the individuals involved. I said yes and was impressed to see that he had a roster of every representative at the facility—American and otherwise. As I pointed them out, he looked surprised by two of the four Canadians I named and asked if I was sure. I told him, without hesitation, that I was.

His second question was more difficult: He asked me to consider the worst-case scenario I feared involving the Canadian captain. I hesitated, then shared the two possibilities that had been haunting me. The first was that the captain might be homophobic and, with the help of his fellow Canadians, could physically assault me for being gay or bisexual. The second was that he might be a closeted gay person who, again with the support of Canadians #1, #2, and #3, might try to sexually assault me.

The chaplain listened carefully and then responded with calm assurance, telling me he understood my fears and found them entirely valid. Just then, the sergeant knocked on the door. The chaplain invited her in and gave a brief overview of the concerns I had shared.

The sergeant responded with compassion, saying she was glad I had come forward and spoken with the chaplain. She firmly agreed that I needed to file an official report. She explained that I could submit it anonymously or with my name attached, but warned that if I chose to identify myself, that decision would be final. I told her I wished to stay anonymous. The chaplain noted that while he supported my choice, anonymity might offer little protection in this case. The captain would recognize the details and realize I was the source of the report. Still, I reaffirmed my decision.

The sergeant respected my wishes and said she would start arranging the process for me to submit my witness statement. She also informed me that, because of the nature of the allegations, she would set up a meeting with Canadian leadership. She explained that the Canadian captain would be placed in confinement and escorted to the main operations building, where the accusations would be shown to him directly. She then asked whether I wanted to inform my team leader myself or preferred that she do it. I told her I would handle it. She said that was fine and offered to be there if I needed support. I thanked both the chaplain and the sergeant. They assured me I could come back anytime if I wanted to talk more.

As I left the chaplain's office and walked toward the main operations building, I silently hoped I would not encounter the captain or any of his associates along the way. Still, a deeper concern lingered. When the sergeant mentioned she would stay behind to speak further with the chaplain, I could not shake the uneasy thought that one—or both—of them did not honestly believe me, despite their words. I wanted to scream that I was not making this up, that I would never fabricate something so serious.

I checked the time and realized I was not ready to go back to the main operations building. Instead, I headed toward the foreign engagement session, an event held most Sundays in the afternoons where representatives from various countries shared the history, customs, and culture of their homelands. On my way there, I crossed paths with the female teammate who had met me at the airport on my first day and helped guide me to my quarters. She immediately noticed the look on my face and asked if everything was all right. I told her about my meeting with the chaplain, that our team leader had been informed, and how I had been told in no uncertain terms that I am being targeted and could be in danger.

She listened carefully and then encouraged me to keep going with the engagement. I had mentioned earlier that I planned to attend. She assured me she would join me shortly, right after stopping at the restroom. I admitted I was nervous that the captain—or one of his teammates—might try to sit next to me. She did not hesitate. "Go ahead," she said. "I will be there before you know it. I will sit beside you and keep them away. I know exactly who they are."

Reassured, I made my way to the venue. But as more American and international personnel filtered into the room, my anxiety crept higher. Any one of them could sit beside me, intentionally or not, and the unknown left me on edge. What felt like a long wait finally ended when my teammate returned, just as she had promised, and took the seat next to me. I tried to concentrate on the presentation, but my focus drifted. More than a year later, I still cannot recall which country hosted the event that day.

After the foreign engagement session concluded, I quickly returned to the main operations building. Thankfully, the team leader was still there. I pulled him aside and fully explained the situation, stressing the importance of speaking to the entire team before rumors started to spread. They needed to hear the truth directly from me—not through whispers or misinterpretations. He agreed immediately and asked when I wanted to hold the meeting. I told him that evening, after dinner, and requested that the whole team be present. He said he would notify the two members assigned to the secondary operations building and have them join us for an emergency ad hoc meeting. Additionally, the team leader informed me that the sergeant needed to see me. I went to her workstation, where she told me that a meeting had been scheduled for that evening—March 10—with U.S. and Canadian military leadership to discuss the situation, and that the captain was currently under house arrest. I thanked her and moved back to my desk.

Later that evening, most of the team joined the team leader and me for dinner. Afterward, we all returned to the main operations building. There, the team leader informed me that the meeting was scheduled for 7:00 p.m. At that point, only three teammates knew what was happening: the team leader, the female colleague who worked in the main building, and the other data scientist. I tried to stay focused on my tasks, but my attention kept drifting to the clock. Each minute seemed to crawl by.

Around the same time, the sergeant pulled me aside and told me that someone else had come forward and accused him of sexual harassment. She explained that this individual had also submitted their report anonymously, but unlike mine, they had not even disclosed their gender. I had left out my name, but indicated I was male.

I began to cry as she shared the news. The night before, I had barely slept; my mind had been weighed down by anxiety, self-blame, and a painful internal conflict. Part of me had hoped I was not the only one who needed to feel validated. But at the same time, I had desperately hoped he had not done this to anyone else. Learning that someone else had come forward shattered me. Through tears, the sergeant gently asked if I wanted to step outside to let it out.

I shook my head and replied, "I am crying because a part of me hoped I was not the only one—but at the same time, I hoped no one else had to go through this. And now that I know someone else did, I wish I had been the only one. No one should have had to endure this."

The sergeant nodded and said my feelings were completely normal in this kind of situation. She encouraged me to try to view it as a positive, however difficult it might be, because now my report held even more credibility.

When 7:00 finally arrived, we headed toward the designated meeting room, only to find it occupied. A supervisor redirected us to a different conference room on the opposite side of the building. As we made our way over, the female teammate who had supported me earlier in the day at the foreign engagement spotted the Canadian captain before I did. With impressive composure, she quickly created a distraction, pretending she needed to show me something, effectively shielding me from crossing paths with him. It did not take me long to realize what she was doing, though in hindsight, I wish I had noticed it even sooner. She executed the moment flawlessly. I thanked her quietly and complimented her on how smooth and natural it had seemed.

Once we arrived at the new conference room, the rest of the team—still unaware of the reason for the meeting—took their seats. I stood before them, trying to steady myself. But as soon as I began to speak, emotion overtook me. I had not anticipated crying in front of my colleagues, and the tears triggered a flood of frustration, embarrassment, and anger at myself. Still, I pushed forward. I recounted the events honestly and directly. As I spoke, I watched their expressions shift to shock, confusion, concern, disbelief, and quiet outrage. Though few words were spoken at first, the solidarity in the room was unmistakable.

4

The Reckoning

Sunday, March 10, 2024, was the day I let the truth out. There was no turning back. My entire team now knew. The only group I deliberately excluded was the Data Team. That decision was not rooted in spite, anger, or a desire for revenge; it was driven by fear. In just under three weeks, I had come to see how deeply the Canadian captain had influenced them. Looking back, I cannot blame them. He had a certain charisma, and many people acknowledged it.

Had the Data Team been included in the meeting, I am sure their response would have been disbelief or even indifference. I did not want to believe it myself—that someone so widely liked could be stalking, intimidating, and sexually harassing a fellow team member. Yet that is exactly what the captain was doing. Why he targeted me, I will never know. It is a question that remains unanswered, and more than a year later, I have accepted that it likely always will be.

The only explanation I can offer is speculation: Either he was sexually attracted to me and, angry about it, wanted to fulfill a fantasy before leaving the facility and returning to Canada. Or he harbored deep homophobia and sought to retaliate violently.

The next morning—March 11—I logged in to my workstation and saw an email from the sergeant, asking me to speak with her about the meeting between U.S. and Canadian military leadership. The meeting had included the Canadian captain I had reported for stalking, intimidation, and sexual harassment, along with two to three other Canadian personnel.

Around 9:00 a.m., I saw the sergeant. She promptly locked her terminal and led me to one of the nearby conference rooms to share the response from Canadian leadership. She said, "The Canadians are requesting a formal witness statement detailing everything the captain did that you found to be stalking, intimidating, or sexual in nature."

I told her I was ready and asked her to let me know when we could begin. I just wanted to get it done as quickly as possible so I could move forward and start putting this ordeal behind me. She agreed and said she appreciated my desire to move on. She then told me she would speak with the Canadian leadership and retrieve the necessary materials to begin drafting the witness statement.

About an hour later, the sergeant returned to my workstation. To avoid drawing attention, she casually chatted with a few analysts nearby before turning to me. She discreetly handed me a small note that read: *We will meet in the same conference room after lunch to begin working on your witness statement.*

As instructed, I went to lunch and then returned—not to my workstation, but directly to the conference room to avoid raising suspicion. The sergeant arrived shortly after with a file folder in hand. She quickly mentioned that she had reserved the room for two hours and asked if that would be enough time. I told her it should be.

She mentioned that I needed to be specific and include dates, detailed accounts, and avoid vague language. She also reassured me that she would stay with me the entire time. Then, she said that Canadian leadership had initially requested one of their representatives to be present during the statement. However, after reading my body language, she convinced them to drop that request.

I began writing.

Each day I described filled an entire page—especially during the first week I spent at the facility. When I reached the eighth page, the sergeant could not help but exclaim, "What all did he do to you?" Tears welled in her eyes as I looked at her and said firmly, "A lot! As I said, he was constantly there." By the time I finished, I had filled ten full pages and part of an eleventh. Of the twelve blank pages she brought, only one remained untouched.

With the witness's statement complete, the sergeant and I continued to sit at the conference table. Before opening the door, she said, "Now we are going to talk about something light-hearted and do our best to get a laugh in. When I open the door, I want you to walk that way"—she pointed to the right— "and I'll go in the opposite direction, so nothing looks suspicious."

We began talking about random funny moments from childhood, teenage years, or our time in college or the military. It was impressive how easily she guided the conversation to something that genuinely made me laugh. Once I did, she smiled and said, "Okay, let's go."

We got up. I turned right down the hallway, and she turned left. Instead of heading straight to my desk, I went outside and into the men's restroom. I took a moment to cool off in a stall, trying to collect myself after everything I had just put down on paper. After a few minutes, I returned to the main operations building.

As I rounded the corner, I noticed the sergeant still in the Canadians' work area. I tried not to look in their direction, but it was hard to ignore the concerned expressions on their faces—they had clearly seen the number of pages I had filled out. The sergeant had mentioned earlier that the other individual who came forward had submitted a one-page witness statement, nothing close to the level of detail or the extent of what I had endured at the hands of the Canadian captain.

After spending most of the day drafting a detailed witness statement outlining the captain's inappropriate conduct since my arrival at the facility, I finally returned to my workstation. I logged in to my terminal, took a moment to reorient myself with my pending projects, and began catching up on emails. Despite the gravity of the day's events, this was still a detailed assignment, and my clients expected timely communication. Unfortunately, I had not had much opportunity to check messages.

Among the backlog was an email from the on-site psychologist, noting her office hours. A glance at the clock confirmed she would be available for the next two hours. I checked her status on the internal chat system—her indicator light was green, confirming she was active. I promptly messaged her, asking if now a good time was to meet, explaining I had just seen her email, which had been sent four hours earlier.

She replied within minutes with a simple "yes." I followed up, asking if I could come by to talk, and again, she responded affirmatively. I let her know I was on my way.

I turned to my team leader and let him know I would be heading to the secondary operations building for a meeting and expected to return within the hour. He nodded. "Okay. We are having a team meeting at 6:30 p.m.—do you think you will make it?" I assured him I would, adding that my meeting should not run long. With that, I locked my terminal and made my way to the secondary building.

I stepped out the door, crossed the street, and climbed the stairs to the psychologist's office, located just down the hall from the chaplains on the second floor of the secondary operations building. I announced myself, and she stood, greeted me with a handshake, and invited me to take a seat.

I introduced myself and explained that the sergeant—mentioning her by name—had strongly recommended I speak with her. I added that I had already met with the chaplain. The psychologist responded warmly and asked how she could support me.

"I'd like to start from the beginning, if that's all right," I said.

"Whatever works best for you," she replied.

I began recounting everything from the start, walking her through each day. As I spoke, anxiety simmered beneath the surface. I did not know how she might react or what she would think. I described the Canadian captain's inappropriate remarks and how he routinely sexualized my body through both words and tone. His voice always changed when he spoke to me, unlike how he addressed anyone else. I detailed the shift in his body language, how he leaned in too closely, violated my personal space, and engaged in unnecessary, unwanted physical contact. I told her about the night he asked if I wanted to go into the bunker with him.

I also explained how, by my second week at the facility, at least three other Canadians began shadowing me around the base—watching from a distance in the same unsettling way the captain had.

As I kept recounting the incidents day by day, I started to open up about the self-hatred and self-blame that had begun to take hold—especially after catching Canadian #2 watching me lustfully while I exercised at the outdoor gym. The gym was located next to the secondary operations building, just across the street and a block away from the main operations center. I described to the psychologist the sudden, sharp fear that shot through my body when I realized what was happening, and how his facial expression changed the moment he noticed I had caught him staring so intently.

I explained how, as I began to process what had happened and considered how to report it to the sergeant, a deep fear settled in. I worried I would not be believed—or, worse, that I might get into trouble for speaking out. I also shared how, after informing the sergeant, my team leader, and the chaplain, each of them asked if I wanted to leave the facility and be reassigned elsewhere for my safety. I told the psychologist I did not want that. This was my first overseas assignment, and I did not want it to be my last.

When I reached the point in my account where I learned the Canadian captain had been placed under house arrest and would be permanently removed from the facility—banned for life from ever returning—I could not hold back my emotions. I also found out that another individual had come forward, choosing to remain anonymous. As I shared this with the psychologist, I began to tear up, overwhelmed by the weight of it all.

What struck me the hardest was the realization that I was not the only one. I struggled to put into words how that made me feel. I desperately wanted to be the only one because the thought of him doing this to someone else was unbearable. Yet, at the same time, I longed for there to be someone else, if only to confirm that I had not imagined it, that I was not alone.

But learning I was not alone did not bring me the comfort I expected. It made everything feel worse. I was not just hurting for myself anymore; I was grieving for the other person, too. I kept asking myself: *How could the Canadian captain have done so little to them, yet so much to me? What did*

I do—or fail to do—that made him think it was acceptable to stalk and prey upon me? Was it because I had been honest from the beginning, making it clear on my first day that I was married to a man, not a woman?

After I gave the psychologist a cue that I had finished speaking, she began addressing each of my questions, one by one. She started by expressing her sympathy, saying how sorry she was that this had happened to me. She explained that she had already been informed that someone at the facility had experienced serious stalking, intimidation, and sexual harassment, but she had not known it was me.

The irony was not lost on either of us. In my three weeks at the facility, I had become quite familiar with her—not just as a psychologist, but as one of the lead instructors for the Saturday fitness sessions organized for the Americans on-site. These classes were designed to keep morale high, especially since none of us were allowed to leave the premises due to the ongoing conflict between Israel and Hamas, compounded by the threat of Iranian-sponsored terrorism, which had made the surrounding environment too dangerous for U.S. personnel to venture beyond the base.

She continued by saying that some questions simply do not have answers, and part of the healing process is learning to accept that. Regarding my feelings about discovering another individual had also come forward, she reassured me that everything I was experiencing—confusion, anger, guilt—was completely normal. I had gone through a traumatic ordeal, and self-blame, she explained, is a common response. Society has conditioned us to look inward first, to wonder what we did wrong, even when we did nothing at all.

She acknowledged that while some people do fabricate stories to get others in trouble, that clearly was not the case here. The details I shared—the clarity and consistency of my account, and how closely it aligned with a witness statement—spoke to the truth of my experience.

Although the psychologist's validation brought some relief, it did not make me feel any better. I still found myself in an internal crisis, frustrated that I had once again allowed my emotions to overtake me and that I had started to cry. She recommended that I schedule a follow-up session with her in about a week and encouraged me to reach out to the chaplain in the meantime. In her professional opinion, I clearly needed continued support, and it was her responsibility to be there for people at the facility. I thanked her, then headed back to the main operations building for our scheduled Monday team meeting and dinner.

Once inside, I checked the time and realized I had spoken with the psychologist for over an hour. The meeting was about ten minutes away. I returned to my workstation, confirmed that the meeting would be in the usual spot, and grabbed my notebook before heading to the designated meeting area. As my teammates gathered in the lounge—an open space in the far-right corner of the main operations floor—I noticed the other data scientist was missing. I asked about his whereabouts, and the team leader explained, "There's an ad hoc Data Team meeting. The sergeant and I requested his presence there. If their meeting ends before ours does, he's been instructed to come join us right away."

During our meeting, we followed the usual routine: each team member gave a weekly progress report, including updates on current efforts and areas where additional support might be needed. When the last person finished speaking, the other data scientist approached and quietly took his seat. Despite his efforts to hide it, his expression looked troubled, and I immediately suspected it was related to the Canadian captain and his sudden removal from the facility. As it turned out, my instincts were right.

Although the team leader did not ask him to recap anything from the earlier Data Team meeting, he did ask the other data scientist to stay behind afterward and provide an update on the team's future. As one of only two data scientists on site, I was also involved in supporting their operations.

As we got up to return to our desks and head to dinner, the other data scientist pulled me aside to share the update personally. He had been one of the few people I had confided in about the harassment I experienced, though I had not revealed who was involved until the previous night. He told me that the sergeant had held an emergency meeting with the Data Team earlier that day to announce that the Canadian captain is being removed from his assignment prematurely.

According to him, the sergeant did not reveal the reasons for the removal, only saying that the Canadian leadership would release an official statement later in the week. However, she did tell them that several analysts from the Data Team had to be urgently pulled from their duties because at least one of them was accused of sexual harassment and stalking. During a search of that individual's room, suspicious items were found—items that should not have been there—as well as questionable internet browsing history on their electronic devices.

The other data scientist added that, although I had confided in him about what had happened between the captain and me, he had not said anything during the meeting that would reveal my identity. I nodded and thanked him. We walked together back to my workstation so I could return my notebook before heading to dinner in the cafeteria. I joined the rest of the team there, while the team leader and the other data scientist stayed behind to privately discuss the earlier ad hoc Data Team meeting.

About ten to fifteen minutes later, the team leader arrived at the cafeteria to eat with us. The other data scientist, however, was noticeably absent. The team leader quickly explained that he would not be joining us. There were urgent matters that needed attention with the Data Team, especially since their operations in the secondary building were now short three members following the sudden departure of the captain and two others. The team leader added that he would be dining with the Data Team instead.

Before sitting down, he also mentioned that everyone should return to the primary operations building after dinner, as a likely ad hoc meeting would be held to address the ongoing situation.

That evening, after dinner, the sergeant asked to speak with me again—this time to give an update on the situation. She told me that the Canadian captain would stay under house arrest and was scheduled to leave the facility within the next 72 hours. Additionally, he had been given a permanent ban from ever returning. The Canadian leadership also released an official statement about his early departure, claiming that he had been called for a more urgent assignment elsewhere and, as a result, had to leave his post in Jordan early. The sergeant stressed that this was the official explanation I should give if anyone asked why the captain left the facility early.

I thanked her and began to turn back toward my workstation, but she stopped me to add that she would keep me informed of any further developments. Once the captain was off the premises, however, he would be in Canadian custody. She also encouraged me to continue speaking with the chaplain, the psychologist, or both, as needed.

I nodded, thanked her again, and headed to my desk. As I walked back, I felt a surge of emotion. On the surface, I was relieved and hoped this nightmare might finally be over. But deep down, I sensed it was not finished yet.

Back at my workstation, the team leader informed us that we needed to head upstairs to one of the meeting rooms on the second floor for a brief ad hoc meeting. This time, the entire team was present, including the other data scientist who had just returned from dinner with the Data Team. The team leader began by relaying the same information the sergeant had shared with me earlier—the official statement from Canadian leadership explaining the Canadian captain's premature departure. According to the statement, the captain had been requested for a more urgent assignment and would be leaving Jordan ahead of schedule.

Although I could tell the explanation did not sit well with some teammates—several of whom clearly liked the captain—I did not hesitate to adopt the official narrative as my own response moving forward.

The next day, Tuesday, began routinely. I logged in to my workstation at 7:00 a.m., and after about thirty minutes, I stepped out to pick up a to-go breakfast from the cafeteria on the far side of the facility. I returned thereafter and resumed work. The air felt increasingly warm and dry, a predictable shift given our desert surroundings.

At approximately 9:00 a.m., the sergeant contacted me through internal chat and requested a meeting. I promptly locked my terminal and headed to her location, aiming to arrive before the foreign partners began filtering into their designated sections on the operations floor. Typically, they arrived between 9:00 and 10:00 a.m.

Rather than speak at her workstation, the sergeant asked me to take a seat on the sofa situated at the center of the leadership area. As I sat down, she got straight to the point: Canadian leadership had submitted an additional request.

Sensing my immediate unease, she quickly reassured me that the matter was not urgent or punitive, but they did require my response by the end of the day. I asked, "What's the request?"

She explained that Canadian leadership wanted to know how I believed the organization should address the involvement of the other Canadians I had named in my witness statement—those I suspected had supported or enabled the Canadian captain's actions. They offered four options:

1. Request their removal from the facility.
2. Request a written apology.
3. Request both.
4. Request neither.

I responded, "Okay, I'll give you an answer no later than 5:00 p.m."

As I returned to my workstation, I felt a surge of anxiety. For some, this might seem like a straightforward decision: Either pursue consequences or let it go. But for me, the choice was far more complex. Three considerations clouded my focus:

1. I did not want to appear petty or vindictive by recommending their removal.
2. I did not want to appear weak or overly forgiving by requesting no action.
3. And I believed a written apology—likely compelled—would be insincere and could breed additional resentment.

After noticing the chaplain was online, I reached out to him. He responded promptly and said he was available to talk. I locked my workstation once again and made my way to his office.

During our thirty-minute conversation, I explained the situation and the options presented by Canadian leadership. Together, we carefully evaluated the implications of each. We agreed that requesting the removal of the other individuals involved was the most appropriate course of action. A coerced apology would lack authenticity and could exacerbate tensions. Taking no action might imply impunity. Most significantly, I continued to feel unsafe encountering them in the facility.

Afterward, I returned to the main operations building and informed the sergeant of my decision. I explained that I had consulted with the chaplain and, after thoughtful consideration, had chosen to formally request the removal of the additional Canadians I had named. I emphasized that their ongoing presence made me feel unsafe, that a forced apology would likely intensify hostilities, and that taking no action would risk signaling that their behavior carried no consequence.

The rest of the day went by quickly and smoothly. Although the atmosphere in the Data Team felt tense—everyone seemed to be walking on eggshells—I decided to act like nothing was wrong. Throughout the day, I noticed the three additional Canadians I mentioned in my witness statement were noticeably absent. In fact, the entire section assigned to the Canadian team looked like a skeleton crew. Where there usually were ten or more Canadians at any time, now only two or three were present. I tried not to focus on it, but I could not help but wonder if they were laying low—perhaps working out of their country's lounge in the building, informally called the "Frat House"—to avoid more attention.

On Wednesday, March 13, I started shifting my focus to the secondary operations building to begin developing the operations dashboard requested by leadership for that facility. The dashboard would be hosted on an internal website exclusive to the secondary operations building and would not be accessible from the main operations center. It was designed to meet the specific needs of the customer—in this case, the facility's senior leadership.

Working from the secondary building made logistical sense because it let me directly code in JSON for the proper internal environment, removing the need to email myself code snippets or walk between buildings to test functionality. Additionally, earlier that week—on Monday—a member of the Data Team (Female Data Team Member #1) informed me that my computer had been reimaged, with all the necessary software installed and ready to use.

This further solidified the need to begin working onsite in the secondary building. I was nearly a month into my overseas assignment and had yet to begin developing the dashboard. It was time to move forward and start fulfilling the customer's request.

Female Data Team Member #2 was athletic and made a habit of working out almost daily. To boost morale within the team, she decided to invite others from the Data Team to join her for a group workout that evening. She asked if I'd like to participate and provided a time that was outside my usual workout schedule, so I agreed to join.

At least four other team members took part, including the other data scientist and Female Data Team Member #1. The workout was refreshing, and for the first time in a while, the group felt more cohesive. People seemed more relaxed and less guarded.

Afterward, instead of heading straight to the showers, I chose to sit and chat with the two male team members who had also participated in the workout—Data Team Member #2 and the other data scientist. It was during that time that an inside joke began to form between me and Data Team Member #2, as I started referring to him as my "emotional support human."

We chatted casually over dinner, covering a range of random topics. Both team members finished eating before I did. Data Team Member #2 mentioned he was heading off to shower, while the other said he wanted to return to his workstation to wrap up a few tasks before calling it a night. I remained behind to finish my meal and, before leaving, grabbed a cup of hot chocolate. I left the cafeteria about five minutes later.

As I rounded the corner from the cafeteria, I spotted the two of them walking in the distance. I continued toward the main operations building to finish out my day. As I walked, an uneasy feeling washed over me, a sudden sense that I was about to cross paths with the Canadian captain. I dismissed it, assuming it was just my imagination.

But as I stepped off the road onto the sidewalk leading to the main building, a black SUV suddenly came around the corner. The front passenger-side window rolled down, and I saw a head lean out. It was the Canadian captain. He waved goodbye.

Not wanting to raise suspicion that I might have been the one who reported him, I went ahead and waved back. As the SUV continued, I watched him roll the window back up and exit the facility for what I could only assume was for the last time.

As I made my way into the main operations building, my mind raced. *Did he not know I was the one who reported him?* I remembered what the chaplain had said: *"As soon as he reads the witness statement, he'll know who it was."* So, then, was he fully aware and simply did not care?

I will admit, I was in shock and disbelief.

When I returned to my workstation, I saw my team leader at his desk and immediately told him what had just happened. I described how the Canadian captain was being driven out of the facility in a black SUV, only to roll down the window and wave goodbye to me. My team leader's reaction mirrored my own—he looked genuinely surprised and said, "Wow!"

Before he could say more, I added, "I am really taken aback by his actions. I keep wondering—was he truly that oblivious, not realizing I was the one who made the report, or does he just not care?"

The team leader replied, "I am sure he knew. You should probably assume he did not care." He added something to the effect of, "He's clearly... something," his tone conveying strong disapproval. He then asked if I had waved back. I told him I had, because I thought that not responding might tip him off—just in case he really *was* that unaware. My team leader nodded and said that was a good call.

He then asked if I had informed the sergeant. I told him no, explaining that I had come to him first because I was still processing everything, but that I planned to go speak with her next. He encouraged me to do so and expressed his sympathy, saying he was sorry I had to witness the captain's departure and his behavior, which clearly showed a lack of remorse or accountability.

I walked straight to the sergeant's desk. Luckily, she was there. I asked if I could speak with her privately about something important, and she agreed. I moved around to her side and asked if she knew whether the Canadian captain was officially no longer at the facility. She shook her head, indicating she had not heard anything.

I told her that he was indeed gone and described how he had rolled down the window and waved as he was leaving.

The sergeant responded with a tone of disapproval, "Really?" I nodded in agreement.

"Thanks for letting me know," she said. "I'll inform Canadian leadership about his actions."

I acknowledged her response and headed back to my workstation. I finished my tasks for the day, logged off, and returned to my quarters for the night.

Lying in bed, I could not shake the image of the Canadian captain's behavior. Why would he wave goodbye to me? Would he not feel ashamed to be removed over accusations of stalking, intimidation, and sexual harassment? I certainly would. Would he not be worried about how this would affect his military career?

Now that the captain was officially gone, I wondered if the other three Canadians named in my witness statement would also be removed. I hoped so.

Later that night, after calling my spouse—as I usually did each evening—to check in and make sure everything was fine, I also reached out to my mom and responded to messages from a few friends who had been checking in on me throughout my overseas assignment. Sometime after, I jolted awake, shaken by a vivid flash of the Canadian captain rushing through my thoughts. For a moment, it felt as if he were in the room with me.

I looked around—no one was there. Still, I could not shake the uneasy feeling that, even if he had not known before, he now definitively realized I was the one who reported him. I sensed a mix of anger, surprise, dismay, and resentment from him, almost as if I were feeling it in real time.

Maybe it was just my imagination running wild, but in that moment, the sense felt all too real.

5

The Slow Healing and Counseling

On Thursday, March 14, I went to the main operations building to start my day, despite my efforts to make sense of the previous night's events. The Canadian captain, whom I had accused of sexual harassment, intentionally bid me farewell, which made me immediately believe he had no remorse for what he did. I stayed focused by putting on headphones and streaming music from YouTube Radio. Mostly, my attempt to find comfort in music worked, even though I kept switching between energetic and sad songs.

It was incredible how dance club hits, love ballads, and break-up songs from various artists spanning the 1980s to the present provided a distraction. Hit songs like Janet Jackson's "Together Again," the Spice Girls' "Spice Up Your Life," and Dua Lipa's "Physical" offered cheerful, upbeat vibes, while songs like Taylor Swift's "Is It Over Now?" and Ariana Grande's "Yes, And?" reflected the thoughts and feelings I was experiencing at that moment. For instance, the latter two songs illustrated my desire to move past the events that transpired during my first two weeks at the facility and accept that everything that happened was beyond my control.

By mid-morning, I decided to find the chaplain to schedule a second visit about everything that happened after our face-to-face conversation. Since he was available that day, I headed straight to the second operations building to discuss the events from the previous night. The chaplain sat back and listened to my thoughts and concerns, including my effort to determine whether the captain knew I was one of the two anonymous people who reported him for sexual harassment and whether his act of waving goodbye to me as he was taken out of the facility was intentional or if he was unaware of the situation.

The chaplain's initial response to my comments about the captain's actions was a single word: "Wow!" He then expressed how sorry he was that I had to go through that and noted the unfortunate coincidence that I happened to walk by just as the captain was leaving the facility for the last time. I explained that if I had eaten dinner at my usual time, I would not have seen him at all. But, to lift my spirits, I decided to join some teammates from the Data Team for a group workout. The chaplain nodded in approval and said that sounded like a good idea, though he reiterated how sorry he was that the incident had happened.

He then asked if I knew whether the other Canadians would also be removed from the facility. I told him I had not received any confirmation about the others I had named in my witness statement, but I suspected they would be removed as well, since it had been part of my formal request—and because I had not seen them in the past three days. The chaplain remarked that they might still be there, but keeping a low profile. He said he would investigate it and that either he or the sergeant would update me. I told him that it was fine.

We finished our conversation with the chaplain, who expressed concern that the delay in removing the others gave the impression that the incident was being treated more like a fact-checking exercise than a credible report needing immediate action. I replied that "I hope that was not the case, although I would not be surprised." I added that at least I knew I was not making things up and that my assumptions about the captain's actions was not an overreaction. The chaplain agreed. I stood to leave, and we agreed to stay in touch as needed.

That afternoon, the three Canadians I believed had been removed suddenly reappeared. A few hours later, the sergeant approached me and asked to speak privately. We walked to a spot out of earshot from others on the operations floor of the main building. There, she told me that the three other Canadians would stay at the facility, despite my request for their removal. According to Canadian leadership, removing that many personnel would jeopardize their mission. They explained that reinforcements would not arrive for nearly a month and that the process could not be sped up.

I told the sergeant I understood. I had already spoken again with the chaplain and had started participating in more group activities, which were helping me cope and shift my focus. She added that if I ever felt uncomfortable, I should come back, and they would consider either sending me home or reassigning me to a different overseas location. Although I nodded in agreement, I felt furious inside. Still, I accepted the situation because I did not really have a choice. I had already decided: I was not going to leave, transfer, or go home. I planned to finish my overseas assignment—I had volunteered for it, after all. I returned to my desk and immediately scheduled appointments with both the chaplain and the psychologist. This time, I started with the psychologist.

In the psychologist's office, I shared not only my thoughts and feelings about the Canadian captain going out of his way to wave farewell as he was driven out of the facility for the last time, but also my reaction to learning that the other Canadians I had named in my witness statement would be allowed to stay. I explained the internal conflict I was struggling with, wondering whether the captain had waved goodbye without realizing I was one of the two people who reported him for sexual harassment or if I had been completely naive to believe he did not know. I also expressed how angry I was upon hearing that the others would stay at the facility. I posed a pointed question: "Why would Canadian leadership ask me what I wanted to happen to the other Canadians listed in my witness statement if there was never any real option available?"

The psychologist assured me that these feelings were normal. She expressed sympathy and offered suggestions for healing. One of her main points was that I needed to accept the fact that some questions—like those I asked during our previous session—might never be answered. She also agreed that it was unfair for Canadian leadership to give me a choice about the removal of the other Canadians if that option had ever truly existed.

Despite acknowledging my anger and feelings of betrayal, the psychologist encouraged me to accept decisions beyond my control. I agreed. Almost two weeks had passed since I filed my official report, and I just wanted to move on. Still, I knew that if I stayed at the facility—by choice—and as long as others who knew and respected the captain were still around, his name would inevitably come up. That would only hinder my healing. And now, knowing the other Canadians I had named would be allowed to stay—under the weak excuse that their removal would "harm the mission"—it seemed certain I would keep hearing his name.

And there was, of course, my desire to learn something from all this despite knowing I had done nothing wrong. Even so, lingering self-doubt and a quiet voice of self-blame continued to burn in the back of my mind.

My one-hour session with the psychologist ended, but before I left to talk with the chaplain, she reminded me that a new psychologist would start next week. She scheduled a follow-up session with the incoming provider. I told her that was fine and agreed to meet next week.

I then walked down the hall to begin my one-hour session with the chaplain. I reiterated the frustrations I had shared during our previous face-to-face conversation just two days earlier. He also agreed that it was wrong for Canadian leadership to offer me an option that was never truly available. The chaplain said he would speak with the sergeant to ensure Canadian leadership was made aware that they should not offer options they had no intention or ability to fulfill.

He ended our conversation by sharing that he, too, would soon be leaving and that a new chaplain would be taking over. However, he assured me that he would still be available for one more week. I left his office and returned to work.

While I could have chosen to confide in just one person—the chaplain or the psychologist—I deliberately sought both perspectives. I've always had some hesitation about placing all my trust in either religion or psychology. In my experience, neither field of thought is entirely reliable, and my tendency to overanalyze and question people's motives often drives me to seek insight from multiple sources. In hindsight, speaking to both—along with family and friends—truly did help.

I kept myself busy by working and taking part in more activities at the facility, including volleyball and touch rugby, both of which were encouraged by the same female team member I had confided in about the captain. She had also sat next to me during the foreign country engagement. I was hesitant at first. My hesitation partly came from not having played volleyball in 25 years—and only during high school physical education—but also from knowing that at least two of the three Canadians I mentioned in my witness statement as accomplices to the captain.

However, once I started playing both sports, I discovered a sense of community and camaraderie I had not expected. I began forming friendships not only with American personnel but also with foreign representatives from New Zealand, Australia, and Great Britain. Gradually, I started to feel more comfortable remaining at the facility.

Unfortunately, during the week of March 25–29, Canadians #1 and #2 started showing up to play volleyball and touch rugby. Their body language was obvious. It was soon clear enough that others noticed their hesitation to join in when I was involved. I felt my anxiety start to grow.

To divert attention from myself, I made a point of encouraging both Canadians to join the games. At that moment, I decided it was best to overlook my discomfort and embrace the unease. I was not going to let anyone's behavior push me away, and I did not think it was worth raising a complaint that might backfire. I did not want it to seem as if I was the one with the issue.

I did not see it as avoiding confrontation, but rather as a decision based on experience. I have learned that confronting others in public often causes discomfort for everyone involved—including bystanders who do not want to get caught in the middle of personal conflicts, especially during activities meant to be inclusive and open to anyone who wants to join.

That same week, when the other two Canadians started participating in the facility's sporting events, I learned from the sergeant that the Canadian captain had not gone back to Canada. Instead, he was living in an apartment in Amman, close to the Canadian Embassy. I could not believe what I was hearing.

It started to make sense why, once Canadian #1 and Canadian #2 rejoined the sports activities, they appeared visibly nervous and hesitant. I remembered seeing them before acting uneasy and repeatedly giving the same explanation whenever someone asked why they had been laying low. They claimed there had been a misunderstanding and that they needed to stay available at a moment's notice until the issue was resolved.

Canadian #1 was the most vocal, saying he could not talk about everything that was going on but would be willing to speak privately later that night after playing volleyball and touch rugby. Immediately, my mind began to race with speculation: Were they going to mention me in that private conversation? Was I about to face retaliation for rightfully reporting sexual harassment? Maybe I was going to have to leave the facility after all.

I could feel my stomach twisting in knots. This week turned out to be one of my hardest during my time there. The entire Canadian team made it clear that their mission was to inform others about the investigation. While I knew my report was supposed to remain anonymous, I could feel eyes beginning to turn in my direction.

Some members of the Data Team—specifically the two female members and one male team member I call Data Team Member #1—began to change how they acted around me. Their body language changed, and they seemed less willing to engage in polite conversation. All three hesitated to speak casually with me and often found reasons to leave the seating area when I was there. When they stayed, they put on headphones and made a point of seeming overly focused on their work.

Proof that I was not overreacting about the Data Team becoming less approachable and more standoffish came from Data Team Member #1. I ran into him on three consecutive days during that week, and each time he saw me, his eyes welled up with tears. On the third encounter, I asked if everything was all right. He quickly replied, "All good, man."

I responded with "Okay," then added that I understood a lot had been going on within the Data Team and that I was willing to listen if he ever needed someone to talk to. He appeared to appreciate the offer at the time and repeated that he was fine.

I kept reminding myself that it was a good thing I had not canceled the appointment with the new psychologist, which the outgoing one had scheduled. I realized I needed it. My anxiety had returned full force after learning that the Canadian captain was still in Amman and that the other Canadians, whom I mentioned in the witness statement, had never actually left the facility. Instead, they had been making frequent trips to the Canadian Embassy and made it clear through their behavior that they resented me. During my session with the new psychologist, I had to bring her up to speed on everything that had happened since my arrival. I found this incredibly frustrating, as it forced me to relive every moment all over again.

Nonetheless, I was thorough in recounting all the events since I arrived at the facility—the unwanted physical contact, sexual harassment, stalking, and intimidation, as well as the ongoing situations during the week of March 25–29. The psychologist was surprised by everything I had experienced and praised my bravery and determination in choosing to stay at my overseas assignment. I appreciated her kind words, but I did not feel brave—in fact, I was starting to doubt whether I could complete the entire assignment. She encouraged me to come back and talk to her again if needed, and she noted that it sounded like I had received good advice from the previous psychologist and the chaplain. She also praised my proactive approach to participating in facility events.

Later that night—Friday, March 29—I went to the paint-and-sip event, which happened every other Friday. It provided both American and non-American representatives at the facility a chance to relax with a glass of wine while painting. For me, it was another much-needed way to keep my mind busy—away from thoughts of the Canadians and the growing worry about what they might reveal regarding my anonymous report. While I knew that the anonymity of my report gave me plausible deniability if any inquiries reached U.S. leadership, I also understood that once enough people spread rumors, it became easier for others to believe they knew who had filed it.

6

The Turning Point

The weekend of Easter Sunday marked a turning point for me. I had started to feel like a victim, but I made a conscious choice not to be one. That day, I committed to taking the rest of my overseas assignment one day at a time as part of my healing. I also decided not to schedule any more sessions with either the chaplain or the psychologist. The thought of starting over with a new psychologist—recounting everything that had happened since my arrival at the facility—was simply too overwhelming. I was done reliving the events. What had happened, had happened, and nothing could change that.

My decision to take this stance was based on a gut feeling. Based on the comments I overheard from the Canadians and their behavior, it seemed they were subtly trying to inform others that the Canadian captain I reported for sexual harassment was probably in the clear. That thought alone made me furious. So, I decided not to dwell on it anymore.

The first test of this new mindset came on Monday, April 1. That day, I chose to work out at the indoor gym behind the main operations building. Within ten minutes, Canadian #2 walked in—the same person I had once caught staring at me with inappropriate intent. I stepped outside to take a quick run around the gym as I considered my next move. Should I go to the gym on the other side of the facility or use one of the outdoor gyms to avoid him?

Ultimately, I decided to return to the same gym and finish my workout, reminding myself that I was not a victim. Although I felt a surge of anxiety, I also reassured myself that the gym had active surveillance cameras, and it would be reckless for anyone to try something inappropriate there.

As I resumed my workout, I noticed him glancing in my direction whenever he thought I was not looking. Each time I turned toward him, he quickly looked away and exaggerated his focus, making loud grunts with every bench press.

I stayed focused on my tasks for the rest of the day. I chose to stay in the secondary operations building for two main reasons: First, the main task assigned to me was only accessible through an intranet platform available there; second, my observations indicated that the Canadians rarely appeared there. I wanted to reduce distractions as much as possible. However, this decision turned out to be more difficult than I expected because the Data Team quickly made it clear that my daily presence in their area was seemingly unwelcome.

Determined to stay professional and maintain good standing with the Data Team, I focused on being courteous and respectful, knowing that my main task required me to stay in the secondary operations building. I also prioritized building strong relationships with the foreign representatives, especially those from Australia and New Zealand. Their friendly, welcoming attitude—and their tendency to call me a "bloke" and "mate!"—made me feel like part of the team.

Preserving these connections became more important. I intentionally worked to strengthen my relationships with Australians and New Zealanders, as well as with selected representatives from the United States and other countries. These efforts included joining weekly morning workouts with Team New Zealand and playing touch rugby with both the New Zealand and Australian teams.

Proof that the passive-aggressive remarks from the Data Team were not just in my head became increasingly clear throughout April. It started when Data Team Member #2 questioned why I always acted so professionally and suggested I should loosen up—essentially calling me a hard-ass without using those exact words. I understood the message. I replied that something had happened during my first two weeks at the facility, but I preferred not to discuss it.

On the night of April 13, a real-world incident occurred that required everyone at the facility to report to the bunkers scattered across the grounds. Earlier that month, Israel had conducted an airstrike in Lebanon, bombing the Iranian Embassy and killing key strategic leaders. It was widely understood that Iran would retaliate, though the scope of their response was uncertain.

That night, Iran launched hundreds of airstrikes that crossed into Jordanian airspace, triggering the emergency bunker protocol. As I sat alone in the bunker, I watched the sky light up in the distance and kept thinking, I hope nothing hits the facility. At the same time, I was worried that if any of the buildings were struck, I was not confident in my ability to apply a tourniquet. That fear was likely magnified by the fact that I was alone.

The airstrikes happened around 2:00 a.m., and many people did not hear the sirens or the intercom announcement telling us to seek shelter. In fact, if it had not been for my team leader—who shared a suite with me—knocking on my door, I might have slept through the announcement too. It was not until ten or fifteen minutes later that three others, still half asleep, wandered into the bunker and joined me. Their presence brought a sense of calm, even though I remained deeply worried that one of those missiles could hit us at any moment. Throughout the ordeal, I saw the sky light up at least a half dozen times. Fiery streaks shot across the night, followed shortly after by overlapping booms and deep, rumbling echoes.

The real-world incident that pushed us into the bunkers probably sparked my urge to confide in someone—other than the chaplain or psychologist—about what had happened to me upon arriving at the facility and what I suffered during those first two weeks before deciding to report the sexual harassment. A few days after the bunker incident, I decided to open up to Data Team Member #2.

He was surprised by what the Canadian captain had done and immediately showed sympathy and concern. He apologized and asked if I had talked to the chaplain, the psychologist, or both. I explained that after confiding in one of the U.S. leaders, she had referred me to both, and I had spoken with them. But after three visits over nearly a month, I decided to stop. I was simply tired of reliving the experience.

He replied, "Good," but added, "After hearing you talk about it, maybe you should consider doing another session with either the chaplain or the psychologist."

I responded, "No, I'm good."

As we continued talking, I could tell he was processing everything I had shared, trying to make sense of why I had chosen him. It felt like he was hinting that I might consider telling the rest of the Data Team, perhaps thinking they would warm up to me or better understand who I was.

I told him it might be best not to say anything, since several team members had been openly upset about the captain's abrupt departure. From his expression, I could tell he knew exactly whom I was referring to. He quickly reassured me not to worry and promised he would not repeat anything I had shared.

While I wanted to believe him, I could not shake the suspicion that he had said something — maybe not directly, but enough to make others suspect I was responsible for the captain's removal.

When he asked why I had confided in him specifically, I said, "You mentioned—before the real-world bunker incident—that you'd be willing to listen, because you sensed something was wrong." He nodded in acknowledgment, confirming that he had said that. I continued, "The bunker incident really got me concerned. It gave me a momentary sense that we could be killed."

He brushed the comment off, saying, "We're going to be just fine. They'd be stupid to target this facility. There are too many foreign representatives from multiple countries. You're probably in the safest place this country can offer."

Looking back, I think part of me still needed to talk to someone, especially as it became increasingly obvious the Canadians were trying to speak with anyone close to the captain. As April progressed, their efforts appeared to gain traction. By the end of the month, during a period of transition within both my assigned team and the Data Team I supported, the Canadians' behavior grew more hostile.

At the same time, the Data Team grew more passive-aggressive, which confirmed my suspicion that Data Team Member #2 had made a comment. He might not have directly said I was the anonymous person who reported their captain, but he probably implied enough for others to connect the dots. Looking back, I see I made a mistake by confiding in him, especially about something I reported anonymously. Maybe I unintentionally prompted the retaliation.

Still, at that moment, I believed the risk was worth it. People's actions always speak louder than words, and the Canadians were already making it clear they were informing those closest to the captain that I was the anonymous reporter. It made sense that they would share that information with the Data Team first. After all, he had been their team leader, and they knew him better than anyone else on the platform.

I noticed the shift with the Data Team around the time the other three Canadians named in my witness statement reappeared at the facility—after keeping a low profile for at least two weeks—and shortly after I confided in Data Team member #2.

Looking back, I realize that filing the anonymous report, the rising tension, and the bunker incident all triggered a deeper sense of fear in me. I suddenly wanted my coworkers to understand the pressure I was under. More than anything, I did not want the Data Team to think poorly of me. Deep down, I knew I had not done anything wrong, even though I questioned myself repeatedly.

Despite my efforts, the Data Team's passive-aggressive behavior escalated. After confiding in Data Team Member #2 at least three times during those two weeks in April, I heard from other team members that they had started calling him my "emotional support human." At first, I did not want to believe it. Later that day, I approached him about the comment. As I vented my frustration, we ended up laughing. In a way, he had become my emotional support coworker.

Amidst all of this, the Data Team was preparing for a Data Camp event, which required full participation from every member. An email emphasized the importance of everyone's involvement. Yet, the team made it clear that my presence was not necessary, which I found odd. As the event date approached, the team's opinions about me began to surface more openly.

The first clear sign that they had figured out I was responsible for the captain's permanent removal—just two weeks before his already-scheduled departure—came during a weekly meeting.

Female Data Team Member #2 (the athlete) and Data Team Member #1 openly stated, in front of the team and several foreign representatives, that they were still in contact with their former captain. They added that he had only provided limited information about why he was removed from the facility.

Among those present was a Canadian representative I will refer to as Canadian #4, a practicing Jew who, after that meeting, started making noticeable efforts to be polite and offer help during the rest of his time at the facility. His change in behavior occurred immediately after the remarks made by Female Data Team Member #2 and Data Team Member #1.

I will admit, I was incredibly suspicious of Canadian #4. His sudden friendliness and approachability felt not only unexpected but also oddly timed, seemingly aligned with my increased presence in the secondary operations building. Of all the Canadians I had seen at the facility, Canadian #4 was the one I had seen the least. He had always kept to himself, more of a loner focused on his work and rarely seen in social settings. His sudden shift in behavior raised red flags for me. Still, I chose to go along with it, largely because I could not get any of the other Data Team members to lift a finger to assist me.

They had no problem supporting one another but showed no interest or incentive to help me in any way. In fact, Data Team Member #1 began conveniently working out of the primary operations building, seemingly to avoid me. This suspicion was reinforced by word of mouth and by comments I overheard when the team did not realize I was within earshot.

The first notable comment after they revealed they were still communicating with the captain came during the Data Camp event. As I entered the secondary operations building, I overheard two female Data Team members passionately discussing, "It was ridiculous he did not come to us about the captain's behavior instead of getting him removed prematurely from the facility!" When I rounded the corner, both women immediately looked startled and quickly ended their conversation.

Within about five minutes of overhearing the two female Data Team members clearly talking about me, Female Data Team Member #2 locked her computer and announced she was heading back to the building hosting the Data Camp. No more than ten minutes later, Female Data Team Member #1 also left the Data Team work area, leaving me alone with two contractors. Both made every effort to focus intently on their computer screens, their expressions noticeably tense, while I chose to pretend I had not overheard anything. There was no point in confronting them. As passionate as their conversation had been, I knew their minds were already made up.

About a week later, another comment appeared, this time from the new Data Team leader, an Australian captain. He asked why I was always in the Data Team work area, suggesting that if I were not there, Data Team Member #1 would spend more time in the space and that the other data scientist on my assigned team could be there more often.

I immediately clarified that I was not intentionally choosing to work in the secondary operations building. I explained that I had been assigned—alongside a data scientist from Great Britain—to develop a visualization platform intended exclusively for leadership located in this building. I also assured him that I would prefer to be seated in the primary operations building, and once the visualization tool was developed and deployed, there would be no reason for me to be there daily.

A couple of members of the Data Team quickly noticed that I had taken offense to the Australian captain's remarks and attempted to reassure me, saying they did not mind me working in their area. But I found that hard to believe, and I made a point of conveying my skepticism through my tone and body language, without saying it outright.

It was clear that the team members who had been present during the captain's comment spoke with him privately, likely informing him that his remarks were insensitive and out of line. He later came over to apologize. While I took the more mature route and accepted his apology, I neither cared nor believed that he was genuinely sorry.

The last week of April and the first week of May were extremely stressful. During these two weeks, five team members left the facility, and new personnel arrived. Among those leaving was the female team member who had picked me up from the airport—and whom I had trusted with the Canadian captain—and also the team leader, the other data scientist, and the female team member who worked solely in the secondary operations building. In addition, Data Team Member #2—whom I jokingly called my "emotional support coworker"—also left.

This change of the guard seemed to embolden the Canadians, who became more vocal in their behavior. Canadians #1 and #2 led the effort to make it clear that I was the one who submitted the anonymous report. The Data Team, especially Female Data Team Member #2, showed her support by helping Canadians #1 and #2 in their actions. Canadians #1 and #2 began to walk closely behind me intentionally, and with help from the Data Team, they made frequent visits to the Data Team work area to admire the farewell plaque the team bought for the Canadian captain—just like they had done for Data Team Member #2.

The Data Team went out of their way to involve the three Canadians I named in my witness statement against the captain who previously led their team. They justified including these individuals by claiming that, unlike other sections of the secondary operations floor, the Data Team area was considered an "open space," and anyone could enter freely. Female Data Team Member #2 (the athlete) successfully brought all three Canadians I named into the space — not only for them to sign the farewell plaque for the captain but also to linger, creating a sense of intimidation and disregard.

The day Canadian #1 was brought into the Data Team work area by Female Data Team Member #2 was the clearest attempt to gauge my reaction to being near one of the Canadians I mentioned in my report. She led him into the space and guided him to the plaque. Standing together, she pointed out the signatures and expressed her feelings about the captain's "untimely" departure. Canadian #1 did not hesitate to speak loudly enough for me to hear through my headphones, saying, "Yes… it's a real shame what happened to the Canadian captain… it was wrong how he was treated and removed from the facility."

Female Data Team Member #2 followed his comment with, "Do you think he'll get the plaque?"

Canadian #1 replied, "Yes, I will make sure he gets it. He will be very surprised and happy."

She responded, "Yes… all of us on the Data Team thought so, too." She then asked Canadian #1 to tell the Canadian captain that we wished him well and said hello, and added that if he needed character witnesses, many of them would be willing to vouch for him.

I chose to ignore the entire exchange, though I could not help overhearing every word. I was livid, but there was nothing I could do. Instead, I kept my headphones on, listened to music, and continued working on the visualization tool, which was more than 70% complete at that point.

Once they finished their conversation, Canadian #1 moved on to speak with other foreign representatives elsewhere in the secondary operations building. As he left the Data Team area, I noticed him glancing in my direction, likely checking to see if I had been watching. I pretended not to notice and kept working. After waiting about 15 minutes, I decided it was safe to leave and head back to the main operations building.

Or so I thought.

Before leaving, I stood up and stretched, casually scanning the open floor plan of the secondary operations building. I saw Canadian #1 talking to someone with his back to me on the far side of the room. Believing the coast was clear, I locked my computer and exited the Data Team area. But just as I rounded the corner, I caught sight of Canadian #1 suddenly turning, finishing his conversation, and heading straight for the exit.

By the time I reached the bottom of the stairs, he was right behind me. As I crossed the street toward the main operations building, I could feel him on my heels. I acted unfazed. I had already decided that the sergeant and my new team leader needed to be informed of what was happening.

When I reached the building entrance, I held the door open for him—he was walking that closely behind me. Though he said, "thank you," I knew it was an intimidation tactic. I made it clear through my demeanor that I was not rattled, that I had gotten him in trouble once, and that I would not hesitate to do it again.

I approached my team leader and told him what had just happened. He had previously asked me to keep him updated after I brought him up to speed on everything I had experienced since arriving at the facility. It was incredibly frustrating that his response echoed what I had heard from others: "Would you like to leave your overseas assignment early or be reassigned to a different one?" As I had told the others, I told him no.

After I described the incident at the secondary operations building, he said, "Go tell the sergeant," adding that he agreed it was ridiculous and in poor taste. As I was about to head to the sergeant's office, he stopped me and asked me to come back for a moment. I returned to my workstation, which was next to his, and he said in a much quieter voice, "Hang on and act like I need you to look something up. The Canadians are watching—do not look in their direction."

I followed his instructions. As I pretended to look at my screen, he quietly described the facial features and clothing of the Canadian team members staring in our direction. Based on his description, I confirmed that two of the four individuals watching us were Canadian #1 and Canadian #2.

We continued to pretend we were looking up information for about 20 minutes, until all four Canadians—including Canadian #4, who was supporting the Data Team—either lost interest or were called away to perform their duties instead of continuing to stare at me from across the room.

Once the new team leader confirmed the coast was clear, I moved to the leadership work area to inform the sergeant. I asked if I could go around her desk and reminded her that she had previously said it was okay for me to share anything unusual I noticed. She nodded and motioned for me to come over. I crouched down beside her desk so I would not be seen and explained that the Canadians had been watching me.

I informed her that the Data Team had gotten a farewell plaque for the Canadian captain and that the same Canadians I named in my witness statement had been shown the plaque and invited to sign it. She asked if I had signed it. I said, "No," and added that I had no reason to do so. She replied, "Good."

I then expressed my concern that they were intentionally implying they knew I was the one who submitted the anonymous report. She responded by reassuring me that she was confident no one knew it was me. I said, "Okay." She also pointed out that there was nothing we could do if the Data Team decided to create a plaque and invite people to sign it.

I replied, "I just find it concerning that the plaque was not only signed by members of the Data Team but also by Canadian representatives, and that it was brought into the Data Team work area with people loudly expressing how poorly they felt the captain was treated. So, before word gets back to you that the Data Team made a plaque for the Canadian captain, I wanted you to know that I am aware of it."

She nodded, and I stood up and returned to my workstation.

The day after the plaque incident there was another weekly partner engagement. During the first part of this event, Canadian #1 was present. Throughout the activity, he repeatedly tried to intimidate me and provoke a reaction by making unsettling comments, including, "Why are you standing so far away... are you afraid to get near me?" I told my new team leader about the interaction and asked him to note the date and time of the incident. I also made it clear that I would be attending the event and expected Canadian #1 to say nothing further, or the team leader would need to step in. Although my new team leader was completely different from the one in place when I first arrived, he was still a strong leader and protective of everyone on his team.

As promised, at least three members of my primary team showed up for the partner engagement the following week. It was uneventful, and Canadian #1, upon seeing my new team leader and two other team members present, kept his distance. At the end of the event, my new team leader approached me and asked if the guy wearing the hat was Canadian #1. I confirmed that it was. He then mentioned that he had spoken with him earlier in the week. Although he could not clearly see their faces from across the main operations building floor, he noted that Canadian #1 had acted noticeably skittish around him and the other team member during a meeting. He added, "We"—gesturing to the geospatial analyst, the other data scientist, and himself— "found him to be unusual, and now we understand why." Before leaving, the team leader said, "We had fun and will probably do it again—and, hopefully, you won't have any more problems."

The following week, after convincing my new team leader to participate in the partner engagement activities—something he had sworn he hated doing—the original group of Canadians who had arrived at the facility as one team was preparing to leave. About two weeks before their departure, Canadian #4, along with some newly arrived Canadians, persuaded me to join their regular Friday partner engagements. I agreed, encouraged by Canadian #4's well-timed politeness and his invitation one evening to join him and a few other Canadian and Data Team members for a Jewish dinner. I decided to attend, thinking at that point that my earlier suspicions about Canadian #4's sudden friendliness were unfounded.

However, immediately after the partner engagement, Canadian #4 made remarks that echoed those of the Canadian captain, which I had reported, instantly igniting a sense of internal outrage. The outrage stemmed not just from what he said, but from my self-doubt: I had initially dismissed my instincts, telling myself I was overreacting when his sudden friendliness appeared conveniently timed. But I later realized my first instinct had been right. It was the smirk on his face that gave it away, a smirk reminiscent of Canadian #1, who had made it clear he was testing me, trying to provoke a negative reaction.

Furthermore, Canadian #4's tone and body language strongly suggested he knew I was the anonymous reporter. The passive-aggressive comments he made on his final day at the facility included: "Perhaps you should move to Canada and be closer to all of us Canadians... Have you ever dated or considered dating a Canadian? Some Canadians on Team Canada like you, and we Canadians—or at least I—are not out to harm you... I look forward to the book you will write about this place."

I was livid. Still, I quickly shrugged it off and responded, "I'm sure not all Canadians are bad, but like everywhere else, there are some bad eggs." I followed up by saying, "I enjoy where I live and have no intention of leaving my job to relocate to Canada."

My shift ended a few hours later. As I walked back to my quarters—night falling and the workday behind me—I could not stop replaying what Canadian #4 had said. The similarities to what the Canadian captain had previously commented on felt intentional, and I could feel my anxiety rising. I knew Canadian #4 did not like me that way; he was not doing the same things the captain had done. He was not engaging in unwanted touching like the Canadian captain had. Still, my anxiety was taking over. I could not stop thinking about it, even as I told myself to stop being so hard on myself.

It was becoming increasingly clear that the Canadian captain, along with the other three Canadians I named in my witness statement, had succeeded in convincing other military and non-military personnel from Canada that he was innocent and that I was the problem. I knew that was not true. Nor did I believe it was my responsibility to make people believe me. Yet here I was, lying in my room, desperately wishing people understood that I would never accuse someone of something they did not do. If I report wrongdoing, it is because it did happen.

Memorial Day weekend arrived, and I knew that in just one month, I would be leaving the facility after completing my four-month overseas assignment. I also realized that the Canadians who had been there when I arrived, including the three I mentioned in my witness statement, as well as suspicious Canadian #4, had already left the facility. I understood I would not see any of them for the rest of my time there. I started thinking about how much peace I would feel knowing they were gone, which my new team leader also echoed.

7

The Home Stretch

The departure of the original Canadians, even with their replacements already at the facility, did not give me a sense of peace. These new Canadians were initially polite during introductions, but they only confirmed my suspicion that the Canadian captain—and the three others who had enabled his behavior—had informed their replacements about me. The new Canadian leader, whom I believe was either a lieutenant colonel or a major, showed no hesitation during our introduction. When my team leader introduced me, he looked me directly in the eyes, shook my hand, and said, "Yes, we know all about you!"

I played it cool, but I knew exactly what that meant.

After we walked away, my new team leader asked if I was sure I had made the report anonymously. I said, "Yes." The problem was that the details in my witness statement probably made it clear who had submitted it. He nodded in acknowledgment, but the look on his face told me he also suspected the word had gotten out, and he was silently warning me to be careful. I told him I would do my best.

Throughout the first week, the new Canadians operated independently at the facility. At least three of them refused to engage in conversation. They avoided me at all costs, including the Canadian operations leader, who had only remarked that he "knew all about me." This was, of course, fine with me. I already had my guard up, and being someone who is naturally not very trusting made it even more difficult for me to place faith in anyone.

It did not take long for other foreign representatives at the facility to notice the new Canadians' reluctance to participate in any partner activities in which I was involved. While I had no problem maintaining professionalism—or what some might call "taking the high road"—I could still feel the tension in the air.

One example of this tension occurred during a morale-boosting touch rugby game, led by representatives from New Zealand who had taken over from the Australians. A captain in the New Zealand military, originally from Great Britain, invited the Canadian leader to play. This was the same leader who, about two weeks prior, had stated in a passive-aggressive tone that he "knew all about me." The captain managed to convince him to join the game, which turned out to be the only time he participated during my remaining stay at the facility.

The awkwardness quickly became apparent to other foreign representatives. Still, I acted as if nothing was wrong, showing eagerness to play and have fun with everyone on the field. I would like to think this helped, but I am certain the occasional exchanged glances, passive-aggressive body language from the Canadian leader, and cutting remarks from a few of the other new Canadians who were bold enough to speak at me contributed to the discomfort.

As the game went on, I noticed teammates subtly making sure their chances of crossing paths with me while on the field were minimal. On one hand, I did not think that was necessary—but I respected those foreign representatives and teammates for being the adults that the new Canadians did not want to be.

Despite most Canadians either keeping their distance or acting passively aggressive, there were at least four others who made a point of ingratiating themselves with me. One went out of his way to give me Canadian maple cookies, saying that Canadian #4 had told him I liked them. The other three, with the help of Canadian #4, who left the facility soon after, convinced me to join a game of street hockey. The new female Canadian, who also served as the team's geospatial analyst, and another new male Canadian insisted on having dinner with me at the café as a group.

I admit I appreciated the four Canadians who went out of their way to be friendly—and not in a passive-aggressive manner. However, I also must acknowledge that there was still a lingering sense of caution. At least this time, all parties shared caution.

During dinner at the café, I sensed that the two new Canadians wanted to ask about the incident. The new female Canadian displayed body language that conveyed sympathy. I would go as far as to say she was the only one, whether from the original group or the newcomers, who genuinely believed me.

In hindsight, it is a shame these Canadians were not the ones stationed at the facility when I first arrived. They demonstrated noticeably better behavior and professionalism. They were more mindful because of the trouble caused by the outgoing Canadian team. Regardless, it was a welcome change.

The first week of June arrived! You might have thought I would be overjoyed, but I was not. Instead, starting on June 2, a wave of emotions overwhelmed me. I nearly told my new team leader I was not feeling well but decided against it. There was a feeling that I had completed my overseas assignment, yet the emotions poured out anyway. Even though I had finished my primary project—creating and presenting a visualization tool that leadership showed strong interest in using—I could not help but be overwhelmed by emotion. I fought back tears, doing my best to keep a brave face and stay professional.

After three days of battling these feelings, one of the Data Team members, who had arrived about a month after me, asked if I was all right. I told him I was fine, just relieved that the project I had been working on since my arrival was finally complete. He replied, "You look at times like you are upset." Like Data Team Member #2, who had left a month earlier, this colleague also said, "If there's anything you want to talk about, I'm willing to listen." I told him, "Okay," and went on with my day.

I left the secondary operations building and returned to the primary operations building. The conversation took place around lunchtime, and I wanted to ensure I ate with my primary team. I experienced a mix of emotions after that exchange. On one hand, I appreciated the concern; on the other, I knew I would soon be leaving permanently and did not see a need to explain anything further. Telling someone else would not fix anything with the Data Team or clear the air. By this point, I no longer cared about being part of that team. My main project was finished, and I did not need them anymore.

As I thought about the conversation, I sat in the Oasis—the same Oasis where the Canadian captain had stalked me, strategically placing himself so that he would always notice me before I even realized he was there. As I sat there, I confided in the new female team member on my primary team about the anxiety I felt walking past the Oasis every day, let alone sitting in it, because of that captain.

She told me that what had happened at the facility would eventually fade, that all I needed was distance from the place, and I would begin to heal. Looking back more than a year later, she was right. I am not as upset as I was then.

Reflecting on my emotional state at that time, she tried to distract me by encouraging me to talk about the vacation I had planned and paid for halfway through the assignment. I told her about all the places I was going to visit in Jordan, since we were never allowed to leave the facility except to pick up or drop off someone at the airport.

As we talked for about fifteen minutes, one by one, other members of our team began coming out of the main operations building, ready for lunch.

About an hour after lunch, I decided to return to the secondary operations building. The openness of its floor plan, compared to the more confined layout of the primary operations building, did not feel as suffocating. The fear and anxiety I were experiencing made me want to sit farther away from everyone, and the secondary building, where the Data Team worked, offered the space I needed to keep some distance.

As I turned the corner and entered the Data Team's workspace, I saw that the team member who asked how I was doing—the one who offered to listen—was the only one there at that moment. He looked up, waved, and I waved back. I logged in and sat at my terminal for a couple of minutes. In the quiet, I decided to go ahead and tell him everything that had happened during my time at the facility.

Something inside me said, "Go ahead—you are leaving anyway. Whatever they think about you after you are gone is their problem, not yours." I asked if he was available to talk, and he said yes. I walked over and started explaining why I sometimes looked upset.

The conversation lasted about ten minutes, but the details were significant. I told him that, from my very first day—during my initial introduction to the Canadian captain—I was subjected to two weeks of sexual harassment, stalking, and intimidation. It started with the captain and eventually involved as many as three other Canadians, which made it necessary for me to speak out anonymously.

I also explained the passive-aggressive behavior I began to receive from some members of the Data Team and other Canadian representatives, including at least half of the new Canadians at the facility. He asked if *he* had ever been passive-aggressive, and I told him no, he had not.

As I shared this information, I noticed his eyes filling with tears, which did not make me feel any better. In fact, it made me more uncomfortable. His empathetic expression felt like it might trigger my own emotions, and I have always disliked getting emotional, especially after everything I went through. It feels like weakness to me.

The second week of June marked a turning point. I had worked through the emotional upheaval of realizing my achievement and was starting to unwind. I was determined to stay engaged and kept participating in partner activities, unlike most others who tended to disappear during their last two weeks at the facility. This behavior quickly became an inside joke I created and shared with everyone there.

Whenever someone was in their final two weeks, they disappeared, rarely seen by anyone. I thought it was strange and decided that, unlike everyone else, I would stay until the very end. Over the last two weeks, I joined in on random volleyball games, touch rugby, and street hockey, all after-work morale boosters. The Aussies and Kiwis were especially my favorite people. They often treated me like one of their own.

I kept busy by finishing minor projects. Some of these involved assisting teammates with data science needs, while others focused on writing manuals, reports, and tutorials for new personnel who would begin their overseas assignments at the facility long after I was gone.

During my final week, I completed at least three reports, a 50+-page manual, and a tutorial on how to use and troubleshoot the visualization tool, which was designed to assist foreign representatives in conducting collaborative analytic engagements and serve as a companion to other tools used for forecasting activities and producing trend analyses.

Others at the facility, including leadership, could hardly believe that I had fulfilled my four-month obligation and produced significant deliverables while simultaneously dealing with sexual harassment and retaliation in the workplace. Even I, for that matter, could not believe it, but I did it.

My final Sunday at the facility—June 16, 2024—was my official farewell. Like every Sunday, which brought both hales and farewells, this time it was my turn to say goodbye. Those departing the facility, whether after four months or whatever length of time they had committed to, were allowed to choose a song to mark their departure.

Surprisingly, choosing a song was harder than I expected. Maybe I was overthinking it, or I was not sure it was worth the effort. In the week before my farewell, several people asked if I would pick a song. At first, I almost decided to skip it entirely. But as the day got closer and the questions kept coming, I started to take it more seriously.

I thought about picking an upbeat song about strength or one of the many dance clubs tracks I enjoyed listening to when celebrating an achievement—after all, I was leaving for good. In the end, I chose a love ballad, a song that was not just the most popular love song of my sixth-grade year, but arguably of the entire 1990s: "I Will Always Love You" by Whitney Houston.

Admittedly, the choice had a certain irony. It was not my way of saying I would always love the people at the facility. Instead, it was a symbolic farewell, a way of acknowledging that, despite the sexual harassment I faced during my first two weeks, there were also moments I truly valued. It was a nod to the experiences I chose to keep—like the kindness I received from the Kiwis and Aussies—and a graceful exit that made room for new arrivals eager to take on the mission.

As the song began to play, many people—including my new team leader—immediately wondered who had chosen it as their farewell track. He looked at me and asked, "Is this your song?" I replied, "Yes." He gave me a look and, with a touch of sarcasm, said, "Of course this would be your song."

I was not prepared for what came next: My team leader insisted that I say a few words because of my song choice. I could have declined, but instead, I decided to walk up to the podium and speak into the microphone.

My first instinct was to keep it lighthearted. But as I began mentioning the Aussies and Kiwis and how they had become like family to me, I got emotional in front of everyone. I was embarrassed, but I accepted it for what it was, finished saying what I needed to say, and walked away, wiping tears from my eyes.

My new team leader later apologized for putting me on the spot. I told him it was okay. The only difficult part was that I had accidentally cried in front of everyone at the facility—literally. I added, "What happened… happened." The other teammates—especially the only female on the team—jokingly responded to my acknowledgment of crying by saying, "Yes, you did." Instead of dwelling on it, I did what any mature adult would do: I kept going with the day and brushed it off as something that had already passed.

During the final two days, my new team leader insisted I stop working on projects and focus on transferring all materials to the data scientist who would remain at the facility. I also needed to clean my quarters, return bedding, check in the equipment I had received upon arrival, and pack my belongings.

There was a feeling of calm as I cleaned, packed, and stored my gear. This busy routine made my departure feel real. The day had finally come. I would not say I was happy, like my family and friends eagerly waiting for me at home, but I was relieved. I knew I had succeeded. Neither the Canadians nor the Data Team had managed to chase me away. I stayed determined—just as my parents had taught me—pushing through and seeing it through.

The day I left was bittersweet. My entire team came to see me off, along with the new team leader and the other data scientist, who accompanied me to the hotel where I would stay for the week-long guided tour I booked to explore Jordan. There were many nerves, mixed with congratulatory remarks from the new team leader. He even made sure to remind me that if anything went wrong, I should have no hesitation in calling them, and they would come to pick me up immediately.

I knew they meant it, and I agreed that I would reach out if needed, all while silently hoping it would not come to that. About an hour later, I was checked into the hotel, lying in a comfortable bed in a room where, finally, I was free to come and go as I pleased.

8

The Adventure

Day 1: June 21, 2024

I woke up on my first full day of vacation. As it sank in that I was finally out of the facility, I felt a clear mix of relief and unease. A lingering worry weighed on me: this was my first international trip alone, even though it was guided. The reason was simple: my spouse could not take time off from his job to fly to Jordan for the week-long trip and come back with me. Both of our employers took employee safety and security very seriously, and it had been made clear to him that while he could submit a travel request to meet me—his husband—in Jordan, he should not expect it to be approved. That was understandable, given the circumstances. The Houthi, a terrorist organization which had become the governing authority of the Gaza Strip and orchestrated the October 7, 2023, terrorist attack at a music festival in Israeli territory, had triggered a wave of heightened tensions. This led to multiple travel advisories for U.S. citizens, along with sporadic escalations and de-escalations of military activity involving Israel, the Houthis organization, and Iran.

More importantly, my sense of unease was also heightened by knowing that every weekend—starting as early as Friday—many foreign representatives staying at the facility where I did my four-month rotation were allowed to go into Amman. I could not shake the feeling that I might encounter certain people, especially anyone from Canada or connected to the Canadians—not to mention the constant risk of violence erupting at any time because of regional conflicts.

That morning, I decided which sites I wanted to visit on my first full day of vacation. I reviewed my itinerary and chose to visit places I knew would not be included in the guided tour package. Before leaving the facility, I was given a detailed itinerary and told that, although the tour was guided, I would be the only person in the group. Deciding to take the risk and go ahead with my plans to explore Jordan increased my anxiety and stress. Still, I was determined to end my time in Jordan by seeing the country, and I hoped it would be without any problems.

As I exited the hotel and walked along one of the busy sidewalks in Amman, I was amazed by how many taxis honked to catch my attention. I quickly discovered one of many lessons during my trip to Jordan: honking was a way for taxis to communicate in Amman. If a driver honked, it was their method of asking if you needed a ride.

Knowing little about Amman and the city's colorful, exotic culture, I jumped into the first reasonably safe-looking taxi. Luckily, the driver was knowledgeable and took me to the first site I wanted to visit. However, I soon learned a second lesson about taxi drivers in Amman: They are very savvy with travelers. Instead of driving off to find another passenger, this driver insisted on parking and walking with me, declaring that he would be my personal taxi driver for the entire day.

In the back of my mind, I could not help but wonder how much this fare was going to cost—and whether I was in any danger of being kidnapped by this person I did not know and driven out into the rural desert and killed. Despite my concerns, I did my best to make the most of the situation. He took me to a beautiful mosque connected to a bazaar, where I had the chance to buy souvenirs. At one point, he took my phone from me—insisting on taking photos of me instead of letting me snap selfies. He then urged me to visit the famous ancient Roman archaeological site in the heart of Amman.

The site was hugely impressive. However, I was not used to the heat, and after about four hours outside, I decided it was time to head back to the hotel—and avoid the overly eager taxi driver. On the way back, he kept asking if I wanted to go to the Dead Sea, Petra, or anywhere else I might want to visit. I told him that the heat was affecting me—which was true—but I also felt uncomfortable spending so much time with just one driver. I already suspected the fare would be high.

Back at the hotel, I re-evaluated my plans and did more research on local customs and travel tips for Amman. That is when I learned an important tip: Traditional taxi services are not the best choice for sightseeing in the city. Instead, Uber is recommended. Uber drivers use GPS, take you directly to your destination, and leave you there to explore on your own terms.

After finding a place to eat dinner and returning to the hotel for the evening, I packed my things to be ready for the next morning, when I would meet my personal driver and begin the guided tour.

***

Day 2: June 22, 2024

I awoke as instructed by the itinerary and made my way downstairs with my luggage to meet my driver. The driver was a young, clean-cut Jordanian, polite, and ready to start the trip. With my luggage in the trunk, I sat down and we hit the road en route to the first stop on the itinerary:

a four-hour drive south from Amman to Wadi Rum, a desert protected by the monarchy of Jordan because of its natural wonder, similar to Yellowstone National Forest in the United States.

The drive out of Amman was smooth, although traffic was heavy at times—a reality to be expected in a country's largest city. As we ventured farther from the city, the air gradually shifted so that soon it was less filled with smog and more with blowing dust, characteristic of an arid landscape with sparse vegetation.

Even though I was comfortable in a well-air-conditioned car with tinted windows, I could still feel the sun's heat on my skin. About an hour outside of Amman, the driver informed me that we would make a required stop in another hour at a fully enclosed bazaar to eat breakfast, use the restroom, and browse for souvenirs.

The driver tried to make conversation. I did not want to come across as unapproachable or rude, so I responded politely but limited the information I was willing to share. Who could blame my caution? I did not know this person, and oversharing could be just as risky as being cold and distant—either approach could make the week we were about to spend together uncomfortable.

Engaging in a moderate, deliberate level of dialogue seemed appropriate. I directed the conversation toward a safe topic by asking about the history of Amman and Jordan in general. When he asked about my wife, I simply said she was doing well, choosing not to correct him out of caution, at least until I felt more comfortable. Before traveling to Jordan for my overseas assignment, I learned that it is one of the more liberal countries in the Middle East, with a relatively higher level of acceptance toward homosexuality. Still, I thought it wise to proceed cautiously until I better understood the dynamic with my driver.

At the halfway stop—a bazaar near the town of Hasa, Jordan, called The Castle Restaurant & Bazaar—I got out of the vehicle and let the driver lead the way. I made sure to stay mindful of the country's customs and cultural norms: If you see women, do not speak to them unless they speak to you first. The men tend to be dominant, highly communicative, generally polite, and very protective of their women. When I entered the bazaar, I was immediately struck by the array of ceramic mosaics, which are a significant part of Jordanian culture. However, it quickly became clear that this bazaar was designed as a tourist trap, with many souvenirs nearly identical to those I had seen in shops around Amman the day before.

We spent about an hour at the bazaar, and while it was not unexpected, the level of haggling from one of the shop owners was impressive. At every turn, he tried to show me something only to throw out an outrageous price to see if I would bite, and each time I declined, he tried to appeal to my emotions. Eventually, I settled on two items, firmly stated that I had finished shopping, and told the driver I was ready to leave. We got back into the car and continued on our way to Wadi Rum.

The changes in the landscape as we approached Wadi Rum were breathtaking—and, to a certain extent, otherworldly. The barren terrain gave way to majestic cliffs and wind-sculpted mountains, with the color of the earth shifting from a dingy brown and pale linen to rich shades of red and bronze.

Wadi Rum itself was breathtaking. As I entered the protected park, I was amazed by how quickly the landscape changed. Even before seeing it in person, I understood why this desert was so highly praised, but being there made it obvious why Wadi Rum is often used as the setting for many movies, especially those made in the United States.

At the visitors' center, the driver allowed me to step out and walk around for about 15 minutes to use the restroom and briefly explore the grounds. There was not much to the center itself. However, in the distance stood a windblown, weathered mountain with a reddish texture. An information board provided detailed descriptions of the surrounding terrain and the distant mountain, noting that it had been used as a filming location for Indiana Jones and the Last Crusade. It also explained the mountain's geomorphology, highlighting that it was mainly composed of sandstone and granite, with thousands of years of weathering exposing the iron oxide that gives the mountains of Wadi Rum their distinctive red hue.

I was genuinely surprised to learn that Indiana Jones and the Last Crusade was filmed here. I had been looking forward to seeing Petra—a world-famous archaeological site and the film's climactic setting—later in the guided tour. But now, realizing that Wadi Rum also played a role in the movie brought a new layer of excitement. There was a distinct joy in learning this, knowing I was standing in a place featured in an Indiana Jones film, one of the series I had loved so passionately growing up, always hoping that someday I would get to see these distant, exotic locations for myself.

We got back into the air-conditioned car to head to the campsite where I would spend the night — a Bedouin-style tent with air conditioning. The driver told me it would take about 45 minutes to reach there, and that in roughly 20 minutes, we would stop in the only town within Wadi Rum's protected borders, Wadi Rum Village.

We stopped at a small corner convenience store that had a limited selection of groceries—items you might find in a supermarket, but in much smaller quantities and variety. The store was owned and operated by a polite and welcoming Bedouin man. Although I was not very hungry, I decided to buy a case of water and some snacks, since the driver told me that once we got to the Bedouin campsite, there would be no transportation available to leave.

Wadi Rum Village was small, with simple, functional buildings that lacked distinctive architecture. Most of the structures were light tan with flat roofs. There seemed to be a small market square for trading goods, as well as a mosque or at least a clearly designated place of worship. The village was surrounded by weathered mountains whose iron oxide–rich surfaces glowed with that iconic reddish hue.

The driver and I stayed at the convenience store for no more than 15 minutes. After paying the owner, I returned to the car, and we continued on our way. As we drove the remaining 25 minutes to the campsite, the driver started explaining the importance of Wadi Rum Village. He said the village has about 500 residents, most of whom are Bedouin. However, he also mentioned that a small number of refugees are allowed to live there instead of being housed in refugee camps.

According to the driver, these foreign residents would be considered "illegal aliens" by U.S. standards, and the Jordanian Ministry classifies them similarly. Yet, because Wadi Rum is a protected area due to its geological importance, authorities do not apprehend them, and they are allowed to remain in the village indefinitely. He elaborated that these individuals come from places such as Syria, Lebanon, Nigeria, Somalia, and other parts of the Middle East and Africa.

Still burdened by anxiety from my four-month deployment—and with my guard fully up from the ongoing sexual harassment and threats I had endured from the two Canadian personnel who were allowed to remain at the facility to complete their assignment—I now faced another concern. As the driver listed the countries these residents came from, I began to wonder whether any might be secretly connected to extremist groups or terrorist networks. The area's isolation made me uneasy. I started to scare myself with the thought that a terrorist group could, in theory, raid a Bedouin campsite and kidnap tourists in the dead of night.

I arrived at the campsite and, with help from the driver, retrieved my luggage from the vehicle along with the water and snacks I had bought less than 30 minutes earlier. We walked into the campsite and headed to the main building for check-in. I was so nervous that I completely missed the driver's earlier comment that once we reached the Bedouin campsite, there would be no transportation available.

So, imagine my surprise when, after checking in and just as one of the campsite workers was about to show me to my tent, the driver, whom I had already spent nearly five hours with, told me he was heading back to Amman and would return first thing in the morning to pick me up for the trip to Petra. I told him okay and thanked him for bringing me safely to Wadi Rum. He responded with a thank you of his own and went back to his vehicle.

As I followed one of the campsite workers to my sleeping quarters, I could not help but dwell on the unsettling thought of being out here in the middle of the desert. A part of me could not shake the fear that a terrorist group might raid the camp in the dead of night and kidnap tourists.

But, strangely, that fleeting fear was a welcome distraction. At least it kept me from thinking about the Canadian captain—or his accomplices.

As I walked with a staff member from the campsite who was helping me with my luggage, I took the chance to take photos of the campsite and the surrounding landscape. Although I felt uneasy about being dropped off and left alone, I was determined to make the most of the experience. When I entered the air-conditioned Bedouin tent, I was amazed at how luxurious it was for a tent. It reminded me of the luxury tents seen in Harry Potter and the Goblet of Fire—though on a smaller scale.

I felt refreshed thanks to the air conditioning and decided to step outside again to take more pictures, this time selfies to share with family and friends as proof that I was in Wadi Rum. Unfortunately, after about 15 minutes of wandering around the campsite and taking photos at random spots, the intense heat overwhelmed me. I hurried back to the tent, eager to escape the sun, which made me feel like I was roasting in an oven—like a rotisserie chicken—under temperatures above 40°C or over 100°F.

The sun's heat made it hard to keep the room cool, even with the air conditioner on full blast. Still, it was cooler than outside. At least I had ice-cold water, though the heat inside the tent slowly warmed it. Still, I made the best of it while I lounged, charged my devices, and kept myself entertained until it was time for my Wadi Rum 4x4 off-road movie locations and sunset tour.

I reflected on everything that had happened since February and reminded myself that, at the very least, I was no longer at the facility. I felt safer than I had back then, though I could not shake a lingering concern about being in a country near terrorist organizations known for anti-American sentiment.

Looking back now, it is confusing to realize all the emotional turmoil and torment I went through—especially over a captain who was not worth remembering. He had probably already moved on with his life, thinking very little of everything that happened at the facility, and proud that he was able to walk away without facing any consequences.

It was 5:00 p.m., and it was time to head to the back of the campsite for my 4x4 off-road movie locations and sunset tour of Wadi Rum. The off-road adventure was scheduled to start an hour before sunset and included about six stops. The first and second stops were filming locations for two different movies shot near each other. Star Wars: The Force Awakens was the first stop. Standing in the exact spot where the lead actress had stood in one of her scenes for a photo was surreal. This was quickly followed by another photo op at the location where Matt Damon appeared in The Martian.

Next, the tour guide took me to a Bedouin camp to have tea with local Bedouins, browse their traditional crafts, and pet camels. The Bedouins attempted to coax me onto one of the camels for a paid photo, but I declined. They encouraged me to at least take a selfie with the camels at no cost, which I did without hesitation.

Near the Bedouin tent was the filming location of a scene from the original *Star Wars* movie. I climbed a reddish dune to see the exact spot where Luke Skywalker attempted to find Obi-Wan Kenobi, a scene I had always assumed was shot on a Hollywood backlot or in Africa. But here I was, in Wadi Rum, looking at production stills showing the precise locations where the characters had stood. It was enthralling.

I began to think that the four months I'd spent at the facility, unable to leave, might have been worth it just to see this majestic, almost mythological place.

The final filming location the guide took me to was described as the setting for a climactic scene in the 1962 Academy Award–winning film Lawrence of Arabia. I always assumed that the movie was shot in Egypt since that's where the story takes place—but I was wrong again.

When we arrived at the site, my guide quickly told me that I had ten minutes to walk around before we needed to leave for the sunset viewing spot to arrive on time. Naturally, I did not want to miss that chance—many people at the facility where I worked had told me how breathtaking it was to watch the sun set in Wadi Rum.

I took a few pictures and asked the driver to take some photos of me with my camera, so I would have more than just selfies. Then I got back into the vehicle, and we headed to the spots the driver said offered some of the best sunset views over the Wadi Rum desert.

The sun's light on the red sands and the surrounding worn, rugged mountains was breathtaking to see. Even though I took many photos, nobody could truly capture the feeling of experiencing it firsthand.

As the sun dipped below the horizon, a sudden chill filled the air. I headed back to the campsite for dinner and later rejoined the same tour guide for a nighttime stargazing trip.

The time between dinner and bedtime was peaceful. I watched the few others at the campsite—about twenty people, including children, which gave me a sense of ease. The food, cooked in underground pits (a Bedouin custom), was excellent, and photos and video recordings were encouraged. I sat and ate alone but felt completely comfortable enjoying the dinner offerings.

Unfortunately, the moon was nearly full during the stargazing tour, which made the stars less visible. Still, the guide showed me a trick for capturing them on camera, resulting in some surprisingly impressive photos.

Back at the campsite, I was eager to shower and hit the bed. My worries about terrorists potentially being nearby still lingered in my mind. Out of a somewhat foolish precaution, I placed my luggage in front of the tent door, thinking that if someone tried to break in, they would trip over it.

The humor of this logic hit me around 2:00 a.m. when I woke up to use the restroom and remembered I was in a tent. If a group of terrorists wanted to kidnap me at night, all they would need to do is cut open the tent with a knife or sword and take me. My strategically placed luggage would not save me.

I laughed quietly at my foolishness and went back to sleep, telling myself not to worry—nothing bad was going to happen. Fortunately, I listened to my voice of reason, quickly drifted off, and woke up the next morning—alive and ready for breakfast.

***

Day 3: June 23, 2024

After breakfast, I quickly walked to the backside of the campsite for my 90-minute prepaid camel ride—my final excursion in Wadi Rum.

As the man leading two camels approached, I could tell he was not originally from Jordan, nor did he appear to be of Jordanian ancestry. While the thought of asking about his background crossed my mind, I decided to refrain. I figured that if he wanted to share, he would.

As he helped me onto the camel, he introduced himself and told me the name he preferred to be called. He mentioned that he was from Nigeria. He was polite and respectfully quiet, quickly picking up on my eagerness to record videos while on the camel.

As we traveled through the Wadi Rum desert—a landscape too vast to see all at once—I started thinking about my spouse and how incredible it would have been to share this stunning place with him. Instead of getting upset, I kept recording more videos, telling where I was and describing Wadi Rum as the natural wonder it truly is.

I have to admit, there was something spiritual and awe-inspiring about Wadi Rum. I felt very grateful for the Aussies and Kiwis I befriended during my overseas assignment at the facility.

Unfortunately, thinking of them also made me think of the Canadians, which I admit with a bit of embarrassment and regret. While I was truly exhilarated by the beauty of Wadi Rum and everything it offered, thoughts of the Canadians—especially the captain and his accomplices—brought a lingering feeling of apprehension and even disgust.

Back at the campsite, I quickly packed up the items I had used the night before and that morning, then made my way to the front of the camp to be picked up by my driver, who would be with me for the entire duration of my vacation.

The next stop was Petra.

Out of all the places on my itinerary, this was the one I had been looking forward to the most. My excitement had little to do with the foreign representatives I had worked with at the facility during my overseas assignment, all of whom had visited Petra at least once during my four-month rotation. Instead, it was because arguably my favorite Hollywood film character, Indiana Jones, had been there in the third film, Indiana Jones and the Last Crusade.

That movie was in theaters when I was in third grade, and even back then, I hoped that someday, as an adult, I would get the chance to see Petra myself. The idea of experiencing Petra in person felt not only exciting but also transcendent and euphoric.

These thoughts raced through my mind as I headed toward the front of the campsite, where I was supposed to meet the driver in about 15 minutes. The campsite, being fairly small, did not take long to cross. As I rounded the final corner, I was surprised to see the driver already waiting, even though I had 10 minutes to spare.

While I deliberately withheld my outward excitement about going to Petra, I eagerly got into the vehicle, silently saying goodbye to Wadi Rum in my thoughts.

The drive out of Wadi Rum was bittersweet. Knowing I would most likely never see that natural wonder again filled me with a quiet sense of nostalgia. Still, I knew, or at least hoped, the next stop would be the icing on the cake.

As we headed to Petra, the driver took a slightly different route than the one we used to travel from Amman to Wadi Rum. However, the landscape stayed much the same—vast, dry, and striking in its barrenness. The driver told me that the trip to Petra would take about two hours, including a 15-minute stop at a roadside gift shop. We soon arrived at the gift shop along the Desert Highway. Small in size, it offered a stunning view of the valley called Wadi Araba—part of the Great Rift Valley that, according to biblical stories, Moses used as a passage to lead the Hebrews to the Promised Land.

The gift shop had two levels. The main floor featured restrooms, refreshments, and handcrafted souvenirs. The upper level showcased larger mosaic artworks and decorative vases, along with an observation deck that provided panoramic views of the valley below.

I stood on the second-floor observation deck as my driver and guide explained the valley's biblical significance and pointed roughly toward Petra. It only took a few minutes for the driver to give some context, giving me a few quiet moments to take photos and reflect.

As I gazed across the seemingly endless landscape, I thought about how much more meaningful this experience would have been if I had been able to share it with my spouse. If he were here, maybe I would have found it easier to ignore the lingering effects of the post-traumatic stress I was carrying from my overseas assignment.

I returned to the car, and we continued to Petra. As the driver took me up the highway—known locally as the Desert Highway—I used the patchy internet connection to learn more about the surrounding area and Petra itself, hoping to avoid being misled into doing anything unnecessary. After about 30 minutes, we arrived in the town of Wadi Musa, the gateway to the ancient city of Petra. Wadi Musa can be described as a hilly town overlooking the Wadi Araba Valley. The driver found a temporary parking spot, purchased my entry ticket—which included access to the Petra Visitor Center, museum, and souvenir shops—and then introduced me to the tour guide who would show me around Petra. He informed me that I had roughly three hours to explore and needed to return to the front of the Visitor Center no later than 3:30 p.m. if I wanted to reach my hotel at the Dead Sea resort on time. I told him three hours would be more than enough and then set off with my Petra tour guide to begin the tour.

We made our way past the souvenir shops, all of which reflected Petra's global appeal and heavy commercialization. It quickly became clear that while most were generic and commonplace, a few offered a slightly more unique selection. Navigating through the rows of shops, where local Jordanian vendors stood outside encouraging tourists to come in, quickly became overwhelming. It's easy to see why some travelers find Petra's entrance experience off-putting.

As we continued along the dirt path, my guide informed me that my tour ticket included a horse ride to the entrance of the Siq, the narrow canyon leading to Petra. Although initially nervous, I was helped onto the horse and began the descent. As we proceeded, the horse handler, who walked alongside me for guidance, noticed I was taking selfies. He offered, rather insistently, to take my phone and capture photos for me.

Less than 500 yards into the ride, I began to recognize parts of the landscape from *Indiana Jones and the Last Crusade*. My excitement took over, and when I expressed my fondness for the film, the handler eagerly pointed out various filming locations along the trail. He even attempted to persuade me to veer off on a horse path, purportedly the same one used by Harrison Ford in the climactic scene where Indiana Jones escapes German tanks to save his father.

Though tempted, I declined, wanting to experience Petra from the ground level rather than from above, and I simply did not have the four hours needed for the detour. It quickly became clear that fully exploring Petra requires at least a two-day pass. Unfortunately, I only had three hours, with about 30 minutes needed to reach the iconic Treasury seen on postcards, and another 30–45 minutes to explore the main archaeological area around it.

About a quarter mile later, we reached the end of the trail and arrived at the entrance to the canyon that guides visitors into Petra. As I rode alongside the tour guide, I was captivated by the archaeological artifacts—priceless relics, many of which, according to the guide, were far too large and significant to be properly displayed in a museum. The guide's detailed commentary enhanced my understanding of Petra, increasing my appreciation for the remarkable culture that once flourished there.

The people of Petra were indeed unique. Though now an ancient and extinct civilization, Petra was, in its time, one of the most important crossroads of the ancient world. It was strategically situated in a region that eventually became absorbed into three distinct and powerful cultural empires. As we made our way through the site, the tour guide effectively highlighted how the architecture of Petran buildings and structures reflected influences from the Egyptian, Greek, and Roman Empires.

There was something euphoric about walking through the canyon. What was most impressive was that I had not yet reached the canyon's end, where the massive building—known worldwide from postcards as Petra—would suddenly come into view. When I rounded that final curve and caught sight of parts of the façade, the hair on the back of my neck stood up, and my eyes widened at the sheer magnificence of this architectural wonder. For a moment, I remembered my nine-year-old self and realized, I did it! I had finally come face to face with something I had only seen in movies, a place I had long dreamed of seeing in person.

There were many people around, yet somehow, I managed to snag a photo with no one else in the frame—I was quite impressed with myself for pulling that off. Near the main building, locally known as Al-Khazneh (the Treasury), numerous local Jordanians were actively encouraging visitors to buy souvenirs or take donkey rides up to the monastery at the top of Petra. One man also invited tourists to climb onto a camel so he could take photos of them using their phones. I could not resist.

There I was, standing in front of Al-Khazneh, the main attraction of Petra, a place I might never see in person again. As the local photographer took photos of me from different angles with impressive results, I felt exhilarated. I was standing where Indiana Jones once stood. When the tour guide told the photographer how much I loved Indiana Jones and the Last Crusade, he pointed out that I was wearing the same shade of boots as Harrison Ford in the film.

Living fully in that moment was thrilling. For at least a few minutes, I had no thoughts of the Canadian captain, his accomplices, or anyone from the facility. It would be safe to say I was in Zen.

After the camel ride, I kept exploring the grounds with my tour guide. We passed a Roman-influenced amphitheater and many smaller structures built on top of each other, pressed against the canyon's red-hued sandstone walls. When we reached the far end of the site, and after turning down at least three persistent offers from local Jordanians urging me to take a donkey ride up to the Monastery, I finally agreed.

The reason for my last-minute decision was simple: The ride would save me roughly 30 minutes of hiking up approximately 900 steep steps to the top of the canyon. With some assistance, I mounted the donkey, while its owner followed behind on another. Together, we began the ascent toward the Monastery.

As we climbed the increasingly steep steps, the donkey I was riding repeatedly edged too close to the brink for my comfort. I could not see the canyon floor below, but I knew that if the donkey slipped, the outcome could be deadly. Sensing my anxiety, the donkey's owner was kind and did his best to soothe my nerves. I asked him for the donkey's name, and he told me it was Coco.

Whenever Coco got too close to the edge, I would shout, "Coco! Coco! You are too close to the drop!" The owner tried not to laugh at my dramatic calls, sometimes shushing me to keep it light. Looking back, I admit it was a bit funny—especially because every time I called out to Coco, the owner would reassure me, "Coco won't kill you; he's a married donkey with babies."

Eventually, we reached the top, where I took several photos in front of the Monastery and the surrounding ancient structures. I promptly declared I would be walking back down on foot—my backside was sore from the donkey ride, and I had no desire to repeat the anxiety of descending the canyon edge on a sure-footed but occasionally unpredictable animal.

Back at the main gate, I was met by my driver, who took me to a required dinner stop before bringing me to the hotel, a resort on the Dead Sea, where I would spend the night.

The drive from Wadi Musa to the Dead Sea took us along the King's Highway, before switching to the Al-Tafilah Highway in the town of the same name and finally connecting to the Jordan Valley Highway. The Jordan Valley—identified in biblical times as the Promised Land—is where Moses led the Hebrews out of Egypt to resettle and begin new lives as free people.

The drive along King's Highway involved a slow descent into dusty desert plains. The scenery shifted from scattered trees and reddish, weathered limestone to dry grasslands and plain, tan limestone soil. With slight variation in the landscape or topography, this part of the trip felt monotonous and dull. Although I was nervous to admit it, I did fall asleep during this stretch of the journey.

The switch to the Al-Tafilah Highway brought some improvement in the landscape as we traveled through the Jibāl ash-Sharā Mountains. The winding road provided more varied scenery, more vegetation, and occasional sightings of native sheep herders tending their flocks.

Driving through the Jibāl ash-Sharā mountains along the Al-Tafilah Highway eventually led us into the Jordan Valley, where we merged onto the Jordan Valley Highway. The scenery at the junction of these highways was breathtaking. By that point, we were going even lower below sea level. The landscape grew more barren and arid—so lifeless that almost no vegetation remained, only jagged rocks and sun-bleached boulders. I could feel the air warming, the sun's heat seeping through the car's tinted windows.

Gradually, small patches of vegetation reappeared as we neared the Dead Sea. These sparse green spots in the otherwise barren landscape reminded me of classic Hollywood desert scenes where a desperate traveler stumbled upon an oasis.

After about 45 minutes on the Jordan Valley Highway, the driver pointed ahead: the Dead Sea. It sparkled brightly against the tan, mostly barren landscape, with dramatic cliffs dropping into the still, shimmering water. Even though the Dead Sea is too salty to support life, it felt oddly refreshing to see.

The driver pointed across the water to the land on the opposite shore—the West Bank and Palestine. Though many in the United States call the region Israel, I did not correct him. It had been made clear to us during training for our overseas assignments that people in Jordan and the surrounding countries do not recognize Israel and still refer to the land as Palestine.

As we drove along the coast, luxury hotels and resorts lined the shoreline. Before taking me to the hotel, the driver stopped at an outlet store. He explained that it offered the same Dead Sea–salt health and beauty products found in the upscale resort shops, but at more affordable prices. I picked up a few items as souvenirs to enjoy with my spouse once I got home.

We arrived at the hotel before sunset. I checked in and got to my room just in time to see the sun dip behind the horizon over the Dead Sea. After having dinner at the resort, I went to bed. As I lay there drifting off to sleep, I felt—for the first time in four months—a feeling of safety.

***

Day 4: June 24, 2024

The next morning, I got up and looked out the window of my hotel room to admire the Dead Sea. I was tempted to go downstairs and dip into the water, a body of water so salty that it allows people to float effortlessly on its surface. I chose not to, but the temptation was strong anyway.

I was able to enjoy the Hilton Dead Sea Resort until noon. The night before, I had booked a Dead Sea salt mud bath for 8:00 a.m. I woke up around 6:00 a.m. and waited for the hotel restaurant to open 30 minutes later so I could grab a quick breakfast before rushing to the spa for my reserved one-hour Dead Sea mud wrap.

I fell asleep as soon as I laid down in the darkness of the treatment room. What felt like only 15 minutes turned out to be more than an hour. Once unwrapped, I glanced at the time to see how much time had passed. I went to the bathroom and washed the mud off in a high-powered shower, making sure to rinse thoroughly before drying off and getting dressed.

I hurried back to my room to change into my swimming trunks so I could relax and swim in the pool, which offered a stunning view of the Dead Sea. Although I only had about an hour to swim, the feeling of Zen and relaxation made me feel completely revitalized.

After swimming, I hurried back to my room to shower, pack my luggage, and check out at the front desk. Within ten minutes, my driver arrived, ready to take me to the next stop: Mount Nebo, a church perched on a mountaintop overlooking the Dead Sea, built in honor of Moses. According to tradition, it was from this very spot that Moses showed the Hebrews the fertile Jordan Valley below, saying to them, "Here is the Promised Land."

The church built in honor of Moses at the top of Mount Nebo offered deep insights into the incredible fertility of the Jordan Valley during his time. It also shed light on the people, the culture, and Moses himself—who, despite leading his people to the edge of the Promised Land, was not permitted to enter. Instead, he spent the rest of his life in solitude on Mount Nebo, gazing at the land from afar.

The self-guided tour around Mount Nebo lasted about an hour. Afterward, I returned to the car, where my driver was waiting to take me to the nearby town of Madaba, a place I had initially planned to visit on a different day. However, because of its proximity to Mount Nebo, I was able to adjust my schedule to include it before being dropped off later at the same hotel in Amman where I had started my vacation.

Madaba is recognized as the birthplace of Jordanian mosaics, and visiting a local mosaic workshop demonstrated how one-of-a-kind each piece is—no two mosaics are the same. The craftsmanship and detail were impressive, with each mosaic telling its own story through tiny, thoughtfully placed pieces of stone and tile.

After the factory tour, I was taken to one of the oldest churches in Jordan, which is home to a famous mosaic of Jerusalem covering much of the chapel's floor. The detailed and careful craftsmanship that went into creating it was mesmerizing. Many Jordanians consider this mosaic the oldest known map of Jerusalem, serving as a testament not only to ancient artistry but also to the region's rich historical and spiritual heritage.

I went out one last time to pick up two days' worth of groceries for breakfast and brought them back to my hotel room. Later, I took an Uber to a nearby restaurant for dinner, then another Uber back to the hotel. I turned in for the night, getting ready for the next day of sightseeing in Amman and Jerash, a town about an hour north of the capital, known for its large collection of ancient Roman ruins outside of Rome.

***

Day 5: June 25, 2024

The guided tour of Amman was brief because I had already visited several spots on the itinerary during my first full day of vacation, thanks to a taxi driver who took it upon himself to show me around the city. The only sites I had not seen were the Roman Amphitheater and Rainbow Street, with the latter being a popular area filled with gift shops, art galleries, street art, and many pop-up markets.

After completing all the Amman stops, the driver continued north to Jerash. The drive revealed a noticeable change in the landscape; unlike the arid central, southern, and far eastern regions of Jordan, the northwestern part of the country was lush with vegetation and even forested areas, a result of significantly higher precipitation.

My experience at the Archaeological Site of Jerash was like Petra: the driver parked, confirmed I had a ticket, and we agreed on a pick-up time. I quickly moved past the souvenir shops at the entrance, avoiding getting pulled in and buying things on which I had not planned. Once inside, the site had two distinct sections: the southern part featured ruins from the Roman Empire, while the northern part dated back to the Greek Empire. This was surprising, as the site is advertised as having the largest collection of Roman ruins outside of Rome. Discovering the Greek influence made the visit even more fascinating.

I spent about two and a half hours exploring the site on a self-guided tour. A part of me had wished it had been guided, since I had so many questions and often found myself at the mercy of the local Jordanian street peddlers. These peddlers were indeed quite pushy, and since I was a guest traveling alone in a foreign country, I did not want to seem too unapproachable or rude.

During my week in Jordan, it quickly became clear how polite and hospitable Jordanians are—though I also noticed a certain level of male chauvinism directed at foreign female travelers. At one point, a young Jordanian street peddler insisted on taking a picture of me with my phone. While I accepted politely, this turned out to be a mistake. Instead of simply returning my phone, he insisted on walking with me and acting as my personal guide—for which I was charged $80 USD.

While I paid willingly—and did get some excellent photos of myself in front of historic and beautiful ancient artifacts that cannot be found in a museum—the situation was a bit frustrating and sometimes unsettling. As we moved from one site to another, I could not help but wonder: Is he going to give me my phone back? Thankfully, he did.

On my way out, I stopped at the gift shop to buy a couple of small items and some water to stay hydrated in the intense heat. I then met my driver in the parking lot, and we returned to Amman.

I spent the rest of the day relaxing at the hotel, only going out for dinner. I was thankful to have made it through the day, especially knowing that the final day of my tour package was completely free. I looked forward to sleeping in and spending the day at my own pace, something I deeply appreciated as I was preparing to wrap up my vacation. I was ready to go home to my spouse, our dog, and the family and friends I had not seen in over four months.

***

Day 6: June 26, 2024

The last day of my vacation in Jordan gave me time to reflect on the past week of sightseeing. I spent part of the morning selecting which photos to post on social media and which to share with family members who were not online. It was nice to sleep in, and around 9:00 a.m., I took an Uber to Rainbow Street, the final place on my list that I had not fully explored.

The street was bustling with people and vendors. The change in pace was invigorating, and I enjoyed exploring the area while contemplating other nearby spots worth visiting. After wandering down a few side streets, I finally reached one of Amman's main roads and walked along the famous Mango Street, where the walls of buildings serve as canvases for local artists.

After over three hours of exploring, I went back to Rainbow Street to catch an Uber to the hotel. I relaxed for a couple of hours before heading out again for dinner—my last night in Jordan. It felt appropriate to enjoy a nice meal to wrap up the trip.

After dinner, I went back to my room and quickly fell asleep. I made sure to get to the hotel early so I could pack and be ready for my 5:00 a.m. wake-up to catch my 8:00 a.m. flight from Amman to Washington, D.C.

I was finally leaving Jordan. Although the one-week vacation had been memorable, I was ready to head home and leave everything that happened during my assignment in Jordan behind me.

***

Day 7: June 27, 2024

I woke up around 4:00 a.m. to be picked up by the driver who would take me to the airport. The driver I had used all week was not sure if he would be the one driving me, so I made sure to tip him for spending the entire week driving me around much of Jordan. Fortunately, it turned out to be the same driver. He thanked me for the generous tip by giving me a gift: a box filled with various cookies and other treats commonly enjoyed in Jordan.

At the airport, I went through customs. I felt a bit nervous because the customs agents were the least polite I had met during my time in Jordan. They insisted on inspecting my luggage at least three times during the two hours I waited to board my flight.

Luckily, I made it onto the plane and was soon in the air. A deep sense of relief washed over me as I knew I was finally on my way home—especially when I landed during a layover in London. Even though England is not my home or place of birth, just being in a Western country brought comfort at that moment.

The three hours at Heathrow flew by, and before I knew it, I was back in the air, heading to Dulles International Airport. I could not wait for the next six hours to pass so I could finally be home. I tried to sleep on the flight as best I could, but flying in coach made it difficult. The flight was fully booked, and there were no available seats to upgrade to first class. Still, I was happy and excited to be heading home.

I landed at Dulles around 8:00 p.m. Collecting my luggage and exiting the airport to wait for my spouse was a quick and painless process—especially in contrast to my departure from Jordan.

Seeing my spouse in person for the first time in more than four months was a relief. Although jetlagged, I was eager to talk to him and hear everything that had happened while I was away. I did fall asleep during the drive home, and despite his encouragement, I felt a sense of guilt. Here I was, finally back home, and I knew he was excited to hear all about my trip.

Even though he already knew what had happened during my first two weeks—and the fallout that followed in the following weeks—and had expressed pride in me for staying at the facility and completing the overseas assignment, he still wanted to hear about my experience firsthand, including the bright moments that did occur.

Nonetheless, he was clear that he also wanted me to get some rest and reassured me that we could talk the next day. He also mentioned that he had a lot to share with me as well.

9

Adjusting to the Home Front

Finally, back home, I found comfort sleeping in my bed despite my jet lag. I no longer had to deal with the hard, thin, full-size mattress; instead, I relaxed on the spacious king-size bed I happily shared with my spouse and our Corgi. Before leaving the facility in Jordan, I had arranged—notably at my employer's encouragement—not to return to work until after the Independence Day weekend. The Foreign Assignment Office advised me both via email and during a teleconference: "Take an additional week after coming back home to the United States off to reconnect with your spouse. Being able to spend time with your spouse will make coming back to work easier after having to deal with the sexual harassment, stalking, and intimidation that occurred during your first two weeks at the facility, as well as the passive-aggressive behavior the Data Team and the Canadian representatives directed at you in the months that followed."

I discussed it with my spouse, and we both agreed it was a good recommendation, especially due to the extra leave I had accumulated. I informed my immediate supervisor of my decision, explaining that it was based on the suggestion from the Foreign Assignment Office. He agreed it was a smart choice, submitted the leave request on my behalf, and informed my coworkers that I would not be returning to the office until Monday, July 8, 2024.

My first weekend back home was on June 29–30, 2024. That Saturday, I attended the local Pride March and the festivities the city hosts each year on the final weekend of June to celebrate Pride Month's conclusion. It was great seeing friends, some of whom I had not seen in six months. The next day, I relaxed and visited a spa for some much-needed rejuvenation.

The first week of July went by quickly, and I planned a long weekend getaway to a beach house about four hours from the Washington, D.C., area, near Ocean City, Maryland. I made it clear to my spouse that this trip was just for the two of us and our dog. Spending that time alone with my spouse was exactly what I needed.

While the beach getaway was enjoyable, I could not shake the feeling of being shell-shocked after spending four months confined to a military base, only allowed to leave for official travel. I knew the only time I truly felt safe was on Saturdays when the Canadians and other foreign representatives were not at the facility. Every part of my emotional self was telling me I was okay. You are back home, safe, with your spouse and dog... Close friends and family are nearby...

And yet, I still harbored a deep fear that the Canadian captain—or one of his three Canadian friends—might suddenly appear as I walked the boardwalk or turned a corner on a quiet street. Of course, that did not happen, but the fear and anxiety felt real, and I found myself frustrated and, at times, angry with myself for worrying about encountering people I most likely would never see again.

On the other hand, the long weekend at the beach also felt freeing. After being stuck in a facility for four months, only allowed to leave for official business, just getting into a car and driving anywhere I wanted, without needing special permission, felt incredibly liberating. There was a part of me that just wanted to drive and walk everywhere. It did not matter where I went, as long as I was moving.

Losing the ability to drive freely for so long, and then regaining that freedom, made me feel deeply grateful in a way I had only ever heard military personnel describe. Experiencing it firsthand gave me a new level of understanding and respect for the people who sacrifice their freedoms and rights so that the rest of us can enjoy ours.

The Monday after Independence Day weekend, I went back to work, caught up on emails, and prepared for a debriefing and close-out meeting scheduled for Tuesday with my employer's on-site medical facility and the Foreign Assignment Office. On my first day back, I received paperwork that I needed to complete before my appointment with the medical examiner. The form asked for details about my physical and emotional health, along with a questionnaire and a narrative section to explain any unexpected events that had happened.

Instead of pretending everything went smoothly during the overseas assignment I volunteered for, I chose to be honest about what happened and how, despite it all, I successfully finished the mission. This included describing what occurred on my very first day at the facility: how I was introduced to the people who made up my team, as well as a secondary team I would support in my role as a data scientist. This secondary group was called the Data Team.

The leader of the Data Team was a Canadian military captain. After he learned I was married to someone of the same sex, it seemed to give him an excuse—at least in his mind—to subject me to unnecessary and unwanted attention. That attention turned into stalking and sexual harassment, which later escalated to intimidation. Over the next two weeks, it became clear that he had begun recruiting other Canadian military personnel to join his campaign of harassment.

Whether this behavior stemmed from an intention to commit an anti-LGBTQ+ hate crime—such as sexual assault—or whether the captain was closeted and trying to force himself on me out of some twisted infatuation, the implication in either case was terrifying. Even as I write this now, both possibilities remain deeply unsettling. The coordinated nature of his actions and his attempts to involve others strongly suggest premeditated stalking, harassment, and intimidation driven by either hate, obsession, or both.

On July 9, I met with the on-site medical examiner to review the forms I filled out. As I described what happened at the facility during my overseas assignment, a worried expression crossed her face—an expression that was unmistakable. I went on to detail the events, and after our one-hour session, she told me I needed to schedule at least one session with both the on-site psychologist and the chaplain before she could close my case.

Despite my hesitation, I went ahead and contacted both the psychologist and chaplain by email and voicemail, knowing these conversations would make me relive experiences I'd rather forget—yet I also knew that doing so was necessary to heal and move forward. After sending the messages, I focused on my regular duties while awaiting a response. I hoped to hear back quickly, but I also understood the need to give them time to read my message and arrange a one-hour session that worked for all of us.

Later that day, I also met with the Foreign Assignment Office for their official close-out. Like the medical examiner, the woman assigned to my case insisted I write an after-action report detailing everything that had happened. Since I was already required to meet with both the psychologist and chaplain at least once, I decided to complete the report. I hoped documenting my experience might help prevent others from going through what I had at the facility. At the same time, I had serious doubts about whether my efforts would make any real difference.

While I was still on assignment, one of my close friends I trust, who has a background in the legal field, expressed deep concern for my safety and started doing their own research. This friend advised me to watch the Canadian military court website, which provides publicly accessible information on court-martials, historical records, and current cases or reprimands. Although I was not particularly proud of doing so, I felt compelled to check the site two to three times a month, starting around April 2024.

I never saw the Canadian captain's name linked to a future court-martial or reprimand. By July 2024, as I was writing an after-action report, I grew more suspicious that the captain who targeted me probably had not faced any profound consequences—no reprimand, no accountability. It seemed more likely that he was simply allowed to return to work as if nothing had happened, despite everything that did.

Having to prepare an after-action report and attend at least one session with both the on-site psychologist and chaplain extended my close-out process by nearly two weeks. While the meetings with the psychologist and chaplain were helpful, they also drained me emotionally. As I recounted each day of my first two weeks—along with the passive-aggressive actions directed at me by the Data Team, the team overseen by the Canadian captain, and his fellow Canadian representatives who stayed at the facility—I felt emotional pain. At least two weeks after meeting with the on-site psychologist and chaplain, I experienced mild panic attacks. On several occasions, I found myself walking down a hallway at work and could have sworn I saw the captain I'd reported, or one of the three Canadians I documented as supporting his efforts, passing me in the corridor. During both meetings, I became emotional, much like I had when I first reported what had happened.

The after-action report ended up being more than twelve pages long. After I sent it to the individuals specified by the Foreign Assignment Office, it quickly moved up the chain of command. During the week of July 22, 2024, I received an email from a senior executive and a colonel requesting to speak with me, separately, about the report, either by phone or in person. I chose to communicate with both via phone and email because I was tired of meeting face-to-face over incidents, and I was ready to move on. Both men wanted to know if I was receiving support from the on-site psychologist and chaplain, and whether I thought my employer should continue sending representatives to that facility.

I emphasized that I was unable to decide whether personnel from my organization should be restricted from participating in overseas assignments at that facility. However, I recommended improvements to pre-deployment training, including a greater focus on the ongoing issues that persist at that specific location.

I explained to both the senior executive and the colonel—who contacted me separately—how quickly I became concerned after learning about the ongoing problems at the facility where I served. These issues seem to recur with each new rotation of representatives and include, but are not limited to, the following:

- One of the buildings at the facility is called the "Frat House" because of late-night parties held there by foreign representatives. These parties led to U.S. personnel being banned from entering the building after 10:00 p.m. (2200) and not allowed to return until 6:00 a.m. (0600) the next morning.
- Routine sexual activity takes place in the bunkers between sleeping quarters.
- I'm not the first person—regardless of gender—to report sexual harassment. I was told I should "feel lucky" for being observant enough to notice the warning signs before the behavior escalated to sexual assault.
- I was also told that sexual assaults have occurred at that facility—not only to women but also to men who have completed overseas assignments there.

While the colonel acknowledged the concerns and assured me he would address them and work to improve training specific to that facility—now recognized as a known risk—the senior executive expressed even greater concern. He followed up by sending an email, keeping my identity anonymous as I had requested, to partner agencies involved in preparing personnel for overseas assignments. The message highlighted the ongoing problems at the Jordan facility, specifically that it is a place where sexual assault, sexual harassment, and inappropriate sexual relations—both with foreign representatives and within national teams—are disturbingly common.

It's hard to tell if any actions discussed by the senior executive from my employer or the colonel were ever implemented. Still, I sincerely hope some improvements were made to the pre-deployment training process. By the time I managed to speak with both the senior executive and the colonel separately, I had already been back from my overseas assignment for nearly two months.

Part of me felt confident that I had done everything I could to raise awareness and voice my concerns about the facility in Jordan. But another part of me had serious doubts. That doubtful part kept returning to the fear that what I experienced would be downplayed and quietly swept under the rug—that the Canadian captain likely got away with it. I also questioned why I was even making the effort when it seemed like nothing would ever happen to the person who targeted me.

I began to understand, on a deep level, why so many women say that reporting often does not lead to much. Why endure the pain of reliving it when the outcome seems predetermined? The incident would be quickly and quietly covered up. And because the perpetrator was in the Canadian military, the U.S. Department of Defense could not compel Canada to take any action against him.

What also made me doubt was hearing how many American representatives—both those stationed at the facility during my time there and those who had served there previously—said that the environment often felt more like a summer camp for adults than a professional workplace. They stated that inappropriate behavior was met with a strict zero-tolerance policy for American personnel, yet it was also normalized—and sometimes even expected—among foreign partners. U.S. leadership seemed aware of this double standard but appeared to accept it as part of the culture.

When U.S. personnel raised concerns about the double standard and the seemingly frequent sexual activity occurring at the facility, U.S. leadership would respond by saying, "While we are the backbone of this facility, U.S. leadership is unable to reprimand or court-martial foreign representatives for engaging in sexual activities—whether those encounters are consensual or forced." This response implied that incidents like the one I experienced would likely continue in the future.

As the weeks turned into months after returning from my overseas assignment, I gradually started to feel a sense of healing. I found comfort in setting clear boundaries and focusing on my work responsibilities during work hours, while dedicating my personal time to my spouse, family, and friends. I reconnected with loved ones in meaningful ways and engaged in team-building activities and collaboration with colleagues during the workday. This included taking on additional responsibilities that required intensive training, which helped keep my mind from dwelling on the events of my overseas assignment.

A job change within my organization also played a key role in speeding up the healing process. Moving to a new worksite with a different mission forced me to adapt to new coworkers, a new supervisor, and an unfamiliar environment, something I had not realized I desperately needed. As I focused on new priorities and assignments, the overseas experience gradually faded into the background. It was freeing not to have those memories constantly weighing on my mind.

Before I knew it, the new year had arrived, and I was nearing the one-year anniversary of leaving for Jordan. What I was not prepared for was the emotional wave that came with it. The week marking one year since I left for my assignment was harder than I expected. A sudden surge of emotions resurfaced, leaving me distracted and struggling to focus. Talking to trusted family members and friends—the ones I wanted to know what had transpired—helped me get through it.

Even though that week was tough, it was not nearly as distressing as the emotions I experienced during the actual events. I could feel myself improving, becoming stronger, and less emotionally overwhelmed by what had happened. In short, I felt I had regained a sense of control, which I have always valued. I have long understood that while I cannot control the actions of others, I can control my own. Not feeling helpless anymore meant everything to me.

Gradually, I began to come to terms with everything that had occurred—both during and after the assignment—especially following my decision to come forward and report the Canadian captain. While I can only speculate about what he may have been thinking, his actions toward me, in hindsight, suggest he harbored a crush of some kind. When things did not unfold the way he may have hoped, it appeared to spark anger, and he seemingly enlisted the help of fellow Canadians to act against me. At least one of them—the man I caught watching me work out with unmistakably lust-filled eyes—seemed all too willing to support his commanding officer.

10

Coming Full Circle

The event that finally confirmed my decision and helped me fully accept everything that happened in March 2025. As I mentioned, a friend told me to check a publicly accessible website that lists upcoming court-martials involving Canadian military personnel. The site includes cases where individuals are charged or reprimanded for conduct unbecoming of their rank. My friend explained that, regardless of rank or the nature of the charge, any official disciplinary action would be listed on the Canadian military court's public docket.

Curiously, after over ten months, the name of the Canadian captain involved in my case never appeared—neither in upcoming hearings nor in past court-martial records. Then, in March 2025, although not entirely proud of it, I asked this friend to send an inquiry email to the Canadian court, providing the captain's full name and requesting information. About a week later, the court responded, stating that there was no record of a Canadian captain by that name ever being reprimanded or court-martialed.

While I had long suspected that his actions had been overlooked, this response confirmed it. My friend was just as outraged as I was—if not more so. They asked if they could forward the after-action report to the Canadian military court to express our shared shock and dismay that the Canadian captain had not been court-martialed for his actions. I told my friend they could share the report, provided all names were removed. This was the same after-action report I had previously shared with the senior executive and the colonel. I also asked them to include a statement expressing concern that the Canadian captain had not been held accountable in any way.

Although my friend never received a response regarding the attached report, simply knowing that someone in the court system likely read it was enough for me. It became clear that nothing had happened to the captain. He had not even received a reprimand. He was allowed to continue his career, his record untouched—something he clearly did not deserve.

Still, I decided to let it go. I know I did everything I could to highlight the actions this captain took against me. And even though nothing resulted from it, I can live with the fact that I tried.

Now that over a year has passed since my overseas assignment, I have had time to reflect on the entire experience, including the extra week I chose to stay in Jordan for a guided tour. Recently, the idea of going on another deployment has crossed my mind.

Overall, the assignment was highly rewarding and helped me build strong relationships with both American and non-American representatives. I feel a sense of ownership over the successes I achieved while at the facility in Jordan. Knowing I contributed to a meaningful mission makes me seriously consider volunteering for another overseas assignment—even returning to the same location despite what happened. In other words, I refuse to let this captain suppress my hopes, dreams, aspirations, and personal ambitions. He may have caused me momentary feelings of self-hatred, doubt, dread, anxiety, and spite, but in the end, he lost.

It is important to understand that just because something negative happened at that facility during my first overseas assignment, it does not mean it could not have happened elsewhere. It could have been much worse. There is a scenario where I might not have said anything at all—especially since the Canadian captain was scheduled to leave the facility within two weeks. If that had occurred, then what? I can imagine being targeted simply for being in a same-sex marriage, even though I identify as bisexual, have been married to a woman before, and still find some women sexually attractive. But when someone learns that you are in a same-sex marriage and knows nothing else about you, it is easy—and fair—for them to assume that you are gay. Since I never mentioned my past marriage to a woman, what else could someone who does not know me be expected to assume?

This kind of introspection boosts my confidence to consider taking on another overseas assignment at the same facility. Despite everything, the living and working conditions are manageable. The facility has air conditioning to provide relief from Jordan's desert heat, and there are several amenities available to help keep everyone engaged during the limited downtime each day.

To be fair, I genuinely hold no ill will toward the Canadian captain or his three accomplices. I hope they are all doing well and have moved on; they have even grown from the experience. Every situation offers a chance to learn something if one is willing to reflect and grow from it.

What I take away from this is that next time, I might choose not to disclose that I am married to someone of the same sex, allowing others to assume my spouse is a woman, since I am often perceived as straight. I also plan to be more direct and assertive in expressing my disinterest in engaging with anyone in a non-professional manner during future overseas assignments, rather than trying to be polite or avoid confrontation.

There is something I must contend with: the understanding that although people may appear more accepting of those in the LGBTQ+ community, that acceptance is not always genuine. We are human, and it is in our nature to want to fit in. While it is encouraging to be liked for who you are, there are aspects of being human that others may struggle to accept or overlook.

Knowing that the facility in Jordan where I completed my overseas assignment is staffed by military personnel from various countries, I realize that the military has historically been one of the least accepting environments for LGBTQ+ individuals. We are also living in a time when many of the rights and privileges the LGBTQ+ community has fought for are being questioned — even by some within the community itself.

While I do not foresee myself taking on a second overseas assignment at the same location within the next three years, if I do, allowing others to assume I am married to a woman might be the wisest course of action. It could help me stand out less and make the experience smoother. Then again, throughout a four-month rotation, the truth might slip out anyway.

In the meantime, I continue working toward the goals my spouse and I share, including our efforts to grow our family through adoption. The adoption process, which had been temporarily paused during my overseas assignment, was quickly resumed when I returned.

I remain dedicated to my journey—to learn, grow, and become a better version of myself than I was the year before. My spouse and I also continue to nurture our shared passion for travel and exploring the world. To both of us, the world is endless and full of wonder, and we find deep joy in experiencing new cultures, trying new cuisines, and broadening our understanding of the diverse lives lived across the globe.

There is so much in life we cannot control, but we *can* control our actions. To the best of my ability, I have made peace with what transpired at the facility and, most importantly, with the individuals who made my experience, especially those first two weeks, so difficult. What happened in the past cannot be undone. Choosing to move forward is the wisest decision anyone can make. I've chosen to move forward.

The likelihood of ever crossing paths with any of the four Canadians I identified in my witness statement is extremely low. I do not live in Canada, nor do I regularly travel there or maintain active communication or collaboration with the Canadian military in my current role. As more time passes, the less likely I am to even recognize them should we happen to cross paths again.

This realization highlights the truth behind the phrase "time heals all wounds." I am in a much better place today than I was a year ago, and I know I will keep growing stronger over time. Already, the facial features of those individuals are starting to fade from my memory. Soon, they will exist only as faint, insignificant snapshots, which is much better than letting them or those experiences occupy space in my mind or life.

The reality is that what happened at the facility should—and does—carry little importance in the bigger picture. Those four months are just a small part of the more than 40 years I have lived. The story I am sharing took place over that brief period, and the year I spent healing shows the slow, careful process that led me to where I am now.

I hope that by sharing this story, others will find the strength to accept what is outside of their control, to recognize that if they came forward, they did everything they possibly could, and that regardless of the outcome, they can be at peace with themselves.

We do not have to forgive those who sexually harassed, stalked, or—worse—sexually assaulted us. While the latter did not happen to me, I know others have experienced it. Forgiveness is not something we owe to the perpetrator. However, forgiving ourselves for any self-blame, shame, or doubt we carry can significantly aid healing.

www.ingramcontent.com/pod-product-compliance
Lightning Source LLC
Chambersburg PA
CBHW051325110526
44582CB00004B/102